Online Arab Spring

CHANDOS
INFORMATION PROFESSIONAL SERIES

Series Editor: Ruth Rikowski
(email: Rikowskigr@aol.com)

Chandos' new series of books is aimed at the busy information professional. They have been specially commissioned to provide the reader with an authoritative view of current thinking. They are designed to provide easy-to-read and (most importantly) practical coverage of topics that are of interest to librarians and other information professionals. If you would like a full listing of current and forthcoming titles, please visit www.chandospublishing.com.

New authors: we are always pleased to receive ideas for new titles; if you would like to write a book for Chandos, please contact Dr Glyn Jones on g.jones.2@elsevier.com or telephone +44 (0) 1865 843000.

Online Arab Spring

Social Media and Fundamental Change

Reza Jamali

AMSTERDAM • BOSTON • HEIDELBERG • LONDON
NEW YORK • OXFORD • PARIS • SAN DIEGO
SAN FRANCISCO • SINGAPORE • SYDNEY • TOKYO

Chandos Publishing is an imprint of Elsevier

Chandos Publishing is an imprint of Elsevier
225 Wyman Street, Waltham, MA 02451, USA
Langford Lane, Kidlington, OX5 1GB, UK

ISBN: 978-1-84334-757-6

British Library Cataloguing-in-Publication Data
A catalogue record for this book is available from the British Library.

Library of Congress Cataloging-in-Publication Data
A catalog record for this book is available from the Library of Congress.

Library of Congress Control Number: 2014955039

For Information on all Chandos Publishing publications
visit our website at http://store.elsevier.com/

Typeset by MPS Limited, Chennai, India
www.adi-mps.com

Printed and bound in the US

Working together
to grow libraries in
developing countries

www.elsevier.com • www.bookaid.org

Contents

List of figures

List of tables

About the author

Reza Jamali is a PhD candidate in Strategic Management at Tarbiat Modares University (TMU) Iran, Visiting Researcher at Radboud University Nijmegen (The Netherlands) and Selected Researcher at Yazd University (2009). He has published widely on issues of strategic management specifically focusing on science and technology ethics, social media and service excellence. His publications include articles in the *Business Strategy* series, *Performance Measurement and Metrics, Journal of Academic Ethics, Journal of Information Ethics* and several international conferences. He is a reviewer of the *Journal of Intellectual Capital, Gender in Management: An International Journal* and *Science & Technology Policy*. Now, he is conducting research on how we can develop an ethical behavior index for social media and the Internet to rank websites based on ethical behaviour, rather than number of visitors. Reza can be contacted at:
Email: jamali.re@gmail.com
Twitter: @RezaJamali1984

Acknowledgements

In conducting these investigations, we have drawn upon the views of many researchers in Iran and some Arabic countries with expertise in such areas as political science, marketing, psychology, social sciences and management, in order to interpret results from various viewpoints. We are very grateful for their insightful comments, which have helped the author to improve the results presented here. We also extend our thanks to Mr. Abbas Imany, who helped us to translate of some sections of the book.

Introduction

We have to start with the most important question: what ignited the interest of the author in researching and writing this book? As is well known, with the initiation of movements and uprisings in the Arab countries and the transfer of the protests to social media, many researchers have attempted to explain the main reasons for the protests in the physical environment as well as in the social media. Because the pace of these changes was too fast, none of these studies could explore the main reasons for the social media's penetration of the protests. In addition, many theories were developed without rigorous research and, in the welter of theories that appeared, were replaced. Because of all this, the researcher concluded that there should be a comprehensive investigation (over the medium term rather than as a snapshot at a specific time). Thus the study began in March 2012 and was completed in July 2014 and was able to reveal the hidden means by which social media leveraged the protests in Arab countries.

This book combines the results of 13 separate studies, large and small, over a period of more than two years. The results of some of the studies are expressed directly in the book, while the results of other studies are indirectly used in the analysis and interpretation of the results presented in each chapter. In total, nearly seven and a half thousand online questionnaires have been collected from seven countries, as well as a number of questionnaires in hard copy in Iran, in order to provide the most accurate results. In most parts of the book, what you see as graphs are the results obtained from descriptive statistics. However, for some of the research presented in the book, inferential statistics also are used and if the results indicate the validity of the descriptive tests, descriptive graphs are included.

It is evident that any research effort, even if conducted in the form of a comprehensive investigation, will be influenced by the attitude of the author. This book is no exception. For most of the time during which this research was conducted the author was in Iran and observed the Iranian people's uprising after the 2009 election results. The author is well aware of the role of social media in the continuation of the protests and a more comprehensive analysis is provided. Nevertheless, if later editions of the book are forthcoming, the author will try to provide improvements in the results and suggestions offered through new and updated research as well as with the help of readers' ideas. For the same reason, we make a genuine request to all readers to share their insightful ideas with the author through personal email.

In Chapter 1, the main objective is to answer the question why social media has had a different penetration rate in different countries. The macro indicators that could affect these areas are presented but we specifically did not look further into these areas. Chapter 2 sets out to present a rational relationship between sociability, social media and national identity. In Chapter 3, we argue that if people feel they have intellectual and economic freedom and that they have a role in decision-making, the level of trust in society will be increased along with security. These cases illustrate the important role of social capital and of how social media penetrates different countries. In Chapter 4, we show that understanding the complexities of the media, selecting the correct source from which to obtain news, and analysing and integrating the news to achieve an analytical result are what have been neglected in the Arab revolutions. Even after the revolutions in these countries, civil unrest with no desired outcome is seen to be a common feature. This is due to problems in media literacy in the Arabic countries. Chapter 5 of the book puts forward the suggestion that, whether we like it or not, the revolutions that have been studied have been formed in an Islamic-Arabic context and cannot be investigated without taking into consideration the religious factor. Therefore this chapter focuses on the role of religion in the media.

Apart from Chapter 2, Chapters 1 to 5 each analyse a specialised aspect of the penetration of social media in the Arabic countries' revolutions. The last two chapters try to look into the two new aspects of social media, i.e. political marketing and strategic management. Chapter 6 deals with three main areas − namely political market segmentation in social media; message design, media selection and message transfer; and feedback and message improvement − in order to provide a new benchmark in this field. Finally, Chapter 7, with its strategic analysis of the revolutions' objectives (social media penetration supporting democracy and the improvement of social justice), tries to offer sound guidelines on how to promote social justice in Arab countries.

The origin of social media effects on countries' fundamental changes

1

Factors promoting social media penetration

What needs to be borne in mind when reading this chapter is that, rather than the *rate* of penetration, it is the *pace* of penetration of social media that is under examination here. For example, although the US has the highest rate of social media and Internet usage, this leading position was achieved not in a short time but over a period of years. However, rapid penetration by the Internet and social media has occurred in the Middle East – especially Arabic countries – between 2010 and 2013; so, all discussion here is centred on the pace of penetration. Moreover, while the role of the telecommunications infrastructure and even the mobile phone is undeniable, the social and psychological factors that can trigger a revolution are also dealt with in my analysis.

Control of the popular media (radio, television and newsprint) by certain world powers is a common thread woven throughout history and countries such as the USA, the UK, etc. use it to induce deep changes in other countries for their benefit. However, this has made us forget the two-sided and twofold effects of social media. It is true that the term 'media' commonly refers to a special group of people, broadly speaking, media leaders; however, when the term 'social' is applied, we can claim that the beliefs, cultures and societal assumptions of certain groups guide these platforms.

This is not be interpreted as saying that leaders of certain social media organisations do not have the power to steer the public – they do. The fact is that the power of the public predominates.

On a larger scale, one may claim that those media developed by western countries to further political / non-political interests in some societies could not only attain predicted goals, but also cut their ties for ever. In other words, the traditional top-down management style (both in business and politics) is slowly shifting towards government by the bottom (where the public have a bigger voice to question and challenge leaders). Thus in this book the term 'social media' will be used for any Internet-based tool where the public mind plays a pivotal role in its development, deployment and governance.

Sense of freedom

The first factor that empowers social media to play a determining role in the revolution is the sense of freedom. When freedom of speech is denied, the social media become a more attractive vehicle through which the public may express ideas. When a post is 'liked' by others, the author may develop the idea that there are people outside his current network whom he or she can lead. From a psychological viewpoint, this imparts a sense that they can be more effective than before. On the other hand, the followers develop the sense that they are not alone in the ideas they hold. That is, in the absence of social media, people may think that their liberal ideas are personal and thus may not reveal them, but it is the calm before the storm. So finding followers to support freedom and making massive networks are features of the social media. Two needs are then met: one is the need for freedom of expression of pro-democracy attitudes and the other is the sense of being seen and having power. Of the five countries studied in this book, Tunisia holds the record for demands for freedom. Social media activists there reported that lack of respect for freedom of speech was one of the important causes that led them to the online social media. Meanwhile, in another part of world, people in the USA tend to use social media as a way to connect with friends, escape routine life and share their hobbies, such as videos, music, photographs.

Concealment

Another point concerning the effect of social media on a public movement is that they can identify the roots of that movement. Looking for a needle in a haystack is an apt analogy, highlighting some positive and negative dimensions. On the one hand, it is not easy for those who might be upset by a public movement to find the trigger point, as many political activists adopt a fake online identity. On the other hand, however, an arrogant government may commission other groups to take control of a public movement and feed it misleading information. The history of Iran's revolution (1978−9) demonstrated social media in the form of flyers with no signature and cassettes that were disseminated as rapidly as their source disappeared. However, what makes Iran's revolution distinguishable from the recent revolutions, between 2011 and 2013, in other Arabic countries, is that the former was not a 'headless' revolution, as the social media were formed and developed in harmony with the goals of one leader: Imam Khomeini. Revolutions in the Arabic countries, including those in the Middle East and North Africa are headless and their leaders, if any, are unknown. One definition of a headless revolution is a social movement with no specific and centralised leadership (Serag, 2011). Lack of a leader brings in worries that the movement might be misled. That is, although social media facilitate the initiation of movements, authoritarian groups may further manipulate the demands of those movements when they gain power. The first step to finding the right path is to identify and distinguish between real and fake revolutionary groups. An intriguing case of the penetration of government-supported groups in social media happened in North Sudan. When the different groups made arrangements to meet each other during demonstrations against Omar el-Bashir, many were arrested by the police forces. The fact was that the regime had penetrated the social networks to find about the future moves of the protesters (Comninos, 2011).

Social capital

This is another aspect of the penetration rate of social media. Because of the importance of the subject, the issue is dealt with in detail in a separate chapter. There is plenty of evidence to suggest that specific high-quality social relations may develop stable and sustainable societies. Sustainable social relations need a high rate of trust in the constituent interrelationships (Jamali and Abedin, 2013). According to the literature, social capital can be classified into seven dimensions, namely: 'group characteristics; generalised norms; togetherness; everyday sociability; neighborhood connections; volunteerism and trust' (Narayan and Cassidy, 2001). Using this classification system, according to my research, trust is the most effective factor in attracting individuals to participate in a network. Trust among members of groups and trust in government improve the efficiency of government expenditures. Trust is a determining factor in the pace of revolution in different countries. Where there is trust among the people and between the people and the government, improvement of general welfare can be expected. On the other hand, when the trust among the people increases between groups and the trust between the people and the government decreases, public power is redirected to social media and extends to the streets when their solidarity grows. There is another situation, which arises when the sense of trust deteriorates both among the people and between the people and their government. In this case, the probability of regime change will increase but divergent groups may infiltrate the movement and attempt to subvert the revolution as the overthrow of the government begins. This was emphatically the case in Egypt. For example, Moaddel (2012) believes that the roots of the movement in Egypt were 'corruption, lack of freedom and police brutality'. Blatant corruption is reflected in the people's deterioration of trust in the government. Lack of freedom also leads to a deterioration in trust between the people and the government, and police brutality is a mark of government efforts to repress social movements and the deterioration of their trust in the people.

Another feasible situation is the development of trust between the government and the public while trust among the people is breaking down. However, there is no instance of this among the countries studied here, and there is probably not enough evidence in other countries. So this last case is unlikely, as revolution, by its nature, happens when trust between the public and the government is diminishing. Another point is that a trustworthy government usually acts as a conciliator when political parties and social groups run into disputes. This is one way that governments add to their legitimacy. My studies confirmed that Egyptian society is split and different groups have lost their trust in one another, though intra-group trust is surging. This situation dictates that whatever party comes to power, the others will line up in opposition. This is because the other parties feel threatened by the possibility of a totalitarian government. This, along with problems caused by foreign powers which add to the challenges, shortens the life of the government. An interesting discovery is that the USA has an average score with regard to trust.

To promote a sense of social trust and solidarity Imam Khomeini used the term 'Basij' (mobilisation) during Iran's revolution. This neutralised the foreign factors trying to divert the revolution from its intended path. Here we can see the role of leadership in the promotion of a sense of trust and social solidarity. As mentioned earlier, however, a headless revolution lacks the factor that creates solidarity and trust. To put it another way, while revolutions in the past were triggered by a leader who was followed by the people, modern revolutions are triggered and powered by the people to bring their preferred leader into power. This is somehow an inversion in the revolutionary process. At any rate, an undeniable feature of social networks is their power to mobilise social movements, the opposition campaign launched in Arabic countries to change the regime being an instance.

Information literacy and media literacy

Another factor which makes social media more worthy of interest is the development of information literacy. There are reports that people in many countries tend to check the news websites in the first few hours of daily work. This hints at the great demand for up-to-date information. Before the expansion of the Internet and social media networks, information was exclusively controlled by totalitarian governments through a system of top-down bureaucracy. People, nowadays, no longer receive information from one source but have access to news sources online that support or oppose the government message. In the past, it was easy for governments to put more emphasis on their achievements and restrict the output of negative news or prevent it from being heard at all. But, nowadays, easy access to a wide range of news, including stories that are highly critical of the current regime, powers the revolution. Dissemination of information regarding the luxury lifestyle of the Mubarak family while many Egyptians live in poverty gradually empowered the protesters in Egypt. Information literacy is now even more critical when we take media literacy into account. According to Martin (2011): 'Information literacy is the intellectual process of recognizing the need for information to solve a problem or issue regardless of setting while working through a process that provides information which fulfills the given need to the satisfaction of the seeker'. But there are some differences to media literacy. Media literacy is more comprehensive than information literacy and is based on Nijboer and Hammelburg (2010): 'The term media literacy is used to incorporate various forms of literacy. The most important are information literacy, visual literacy, textual literacy, new media literacies, and news/mass media literacy'.

Moreover, in information literacy you are only an information seeker, but when you enrich yourself with media literacy, you may analyse and even create data, information and messages. When a society's knowledge fails to improve to a greater extent than its information literacy, the society may not be able to decipher the media's complexity and as a result its culture might be easily affected. Information literacy is not enough for detailed analysis, while media literacy corresponds with the ability to think critically so that one is able to choose between different alternatives. Suppose you encounter this message in a social medium: 'Our leaders are symbols of corruption in the country. We all need to fight and kill them. Killing them is lawful (halal)'. Results from my research show that reactions to such messages are affected by gender and level of education. Women and highly educated people in a study sample tend to post comments on such messages rather than simply 'liking' or 'tagging', that is, they do not jump to conclusions. In other words, they prefer not to decide immediately, and so mostly maintain a moderate approach. Although there is no evident relation between the reaction of an individual and their level of media literacy in such situations, in a later chapter I will show that educated people and those with high levels of media literacy have the capacity to analyse issues from different perspectives and tend to take into account aspects such as justice, aesthetic concerns and even religion. On the one hand, people with greater information literacy alone do not hesitate to accept the message. Although they have a nagging sense of the injustice being done in their society, they fail to see that killing the rulers without taking them to court is also a case of injustice. This makes them nothing but followers and good targets for movement leaders. On the other hand, those empowered with media literacy and highly educated people tend to think about the issues and are not merely followers. An interesting point is that in spite of the termination of the monopoly on information using information literacy, there is still a threat of cyber-monopoly. The first group that lacks media literacy grows, making massive networks, and gradually forms another type of autocratic society where the elites of cyber society are forced into isolation. This brings in to play another issue. As proved by history, the isolation of elites in society and the increase of focus on average people have been among the main causes of revolutions. Thus where the mob is the main power of modern revolutions and movements in virtual networks, apparently the elite will be once again forced into isolation. To break the vicious circle of failure of revolutions, it is critical to improve media literacy among the public and enable people to play an active rather than a passive role in virtual networks. In fact, an effective and fruitful revolution needs an improvement in media literacy in society on a large scale.

Mono-nationality and cultural exchanges

The next factors contributing to the pace of social media among different nations are mono-nationality and cultural exchange. Of the countries in the Middle East, Iran, Turkey and Iraq can be considered multinational. On the other hand, the majority of the Arabic countries in that region are considered to be mono-national. When it comes to social media, there is a dominant culture which feeds the main portion of the material and consequently influences other subcultures – and of course is influenced by them in return. The cultural exchange is a relatively gradual process. However, for mono-national countries, the formation of focal points which appeal to everyone is rather faster. In such a scenario, there is usually no need for fundamental changes as people are quick to agree on an issue and join social groups. The problem of regime is raised when the governing power is challenged by a crisis of legitimacy and national identity. By crisis of legitimacy we are referring to the situation where the ruling power, in the eyes of the public, is deemed to have no authority to rule, which usually results in a gap between the actual system and the preferred one. Such a situation might be a cause or a consequence of the national identity of the people. In this regard the question is about the extent of the acceptance of authority. Do the people find themselves mentally belonging to the system? My research regarding national identity in Egypt, Libya, Jordan, Yemen and Tunisia shows that, in spite of recent revolution and the initiation of a transition phase, people still have a poor sense of national identity. This might trigger the next major movement against the ruling power. It is noticeable that these countries score differently with regard to their national identity and that the different aspects of national identity are not the same in each country. Therefore each aspect needs to be dealt with separately (and is the subject of another chapter). For now, we need to keep in mind that mono-nationality facilitates the formation of massive groups in the social media, and when this happens at the same time as a weak sense of national identity and a crisis of legitimacy, social movements are inevitable.

Soft war

When it comes to social media online, we need to keep in mind that the origins of these media stories are typically in western countries such as the USA and throughout Europe. Therefore it is not beyond reasonable expectations that western countries, to a large extent, benefit directly from these uprisings. They use these media channels to move towards the attainment of the goals they have already made desirable in Arabic countries, in order to increase their power and influence. Thus, when a 'soft war' is waged against a country, social media tend to penetrate at a faster pace. International public relations nowadays are one of the most effective weapons of soft war. Clearly, tools such as social networks play a determining role in this regard.

In the literature we find that the term 'soft power' is actually used more than the term 'soft war'. But in recent years some countries, such as Iran, have extended the use of soft war. Price (2012) noted: 'For the Islamic Republic, soft-war was defined as the strategic and focused use of nonmilitary means to achieve objectives, such as regime change, that might otherwise be obtained through conventional weaponry'.

According to the Arab Knowledge Report (2009), there are approximately 60 million Internet users living in Arabic countries and that number will reach 100 million by 2015; this indicates that there will be more members of the local population online and using social networks who value transparency and responsiveness as a characteristic to be sought from governmental bodies (Ghannam, 2011). The statistics of Internet use are more interesting in Egypt: in August 2010, 5.2 million Egyptians had a Facebook account, and this figure reached 6.6 and 7.3 million respectively in February 2011 and August 2011 (Chorev, 2011) – almost ten per cent of the population. Although ten per cent may not be considered a high level of representation, it does show there is a growing trend in the importance of the role of social networks in the everyday life of the nation. On the other hand, there are also Internet users who are seeking to use the Internet to lead the revolution in search of a better life, so it is a substantial force. The same is true in other Arabic countries. In August 2011, for instance, 24 per cent of Tunisians, 23.6 per cent of Bahrainis, 15 per cent of Saudi Arabians and 29 per cent of Lebanese were on Facebook. However, in countries such as Libya (0.8 per cent) and Yemen (1.4 per cent) a much smaller number of the population are members of virtual networks. The point is, however, that the role such small groups play in social networks is undeniable (Chorev, 2011). While this segment of the population may have no physical presence, can only be accessed online and consists mainly of the youth, who are usually dissatisfied with the status quo, it is vulnerable to soft war. Almost all the features of soft war find social media useful as a development platform:

- *Actors from different groups.* There is a wide range of players in soft war, each imposing a threat to specific social, cultural and political aspects of the society. Of the different aspects, cultural effects are the most evident. One may say that cultural changes are the most effective factors in soft war, as the phenomenon deals with thoughts. In fact, soft power forces rivals to confront each other and shake hands, as they think they are in agreement with the enemy.
- *Avoiding violence.* Whereas hard war features destruction, physical elimination and territorial expansion, soft war moves forward by influencing elections and selection processes, decision-making processes and behavioural patterns so that eventually the rival surrenders (after metamorphosis) by accepting what has been imposed. The problem is that the subjects of soft war — the citizens of a country — fail to see the objectives behind the gradual changes and even evaluate them as positive as they have come to the conclusion that such changes are in their favour.
- *Complexity.* The phenomenon is complicated, multilayered and multi-aspect. It is also hard to measure, as it is the product of the minds of the elite. In the case of hard war, on the other hand, physical appearance and tangible features make it easy to measure.
- *Ambiguity.* Actors in a soft war pose as friends and follow the goals of their conspiracy while pretending to help their rivals. This makes them unnoticeable in the eyes of the public and even to groups of elites.
- *Inclusiveness.* While traditional wars attack a specific group in a society (in most cases the armed forces), soft war deals with all social groups. (Naeini, 2010)

However, thinking that soft war is merely an external factor is wrong, as it may be led by the citizens against the government, which gives it a two-dimensional nature. In fact, when protesters employ soft-war tactics in social media to bring about fundamental changes, they have waged a soft war to lead the masses toward their goals. However, while the ambiguous nature of soft war makes it impossible to devise an accurate measure of the phenomenon across social networks, it is noteworthy that 81 per cent of respondents in the five countries in the study believed that the social media would hold the upper hand in soft war and 39 per cent believed that their revolution was the result of some kind of soft war. On the other hand, 61 per cent believed that their revolution was the will of their nation and had not been triggered by a foreign power; this group also responded that their revolution had not been manipulated by groups other than revolutionary actors and protesters. Figure 1.1 illustrates the penetration of Facebook into Arab countries in 2012, according to the Arab Social Media Report.

Iran, Turkey and Israel are discussed here for the sake of comparison with Arabic countries. However, we point out that statistics from Iran cannot be considered accurate as Facebook is filtered by the Iranian government and there is no accurate data about Iranian users of Facebook – some statistics even report there are no Iranian users of Facebook at all. Figure 1.1 clearly shows that Syrians and Egyptians, by far, constitute the greatest number of new Facebook users in Arabic countries. The greater popularity of Facebook in these two countries is coincident with the protest movements. In the case of Saudi Arabia (KSA), we see a high rate of penetration of social networks; this, along with the rise of information transparency, imposes a more serious threat to the Saudi regime, and this country may well be the next host of the Arab Spring. There are plenty of instances of a surge in the use of social media during public movements in different countries. For instance, Chappelle (2010) reports that on 12 June 2009 during the presidential election in Iran, there were a record 2,500 tweets per hour regarding the result of the election; this level hit 16,000 tweets per hour on 20 June. This illustrates that social media may also be considered a predictive tool and their use can be an alarm signal. When a surge in the use of social media occurs, it shows general agreement among the people and we have to be prepared to see protesters in the streets at any moment.

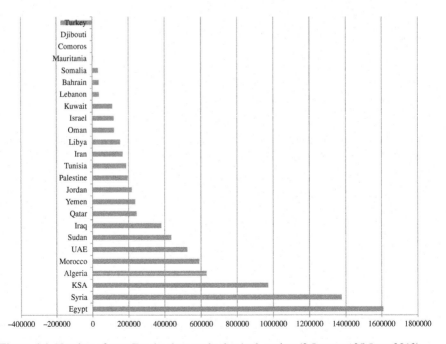

Figure 1.1 Number of new Facebook users in the Arab region (3 January–25 June 2012). *Source*: Arab Social Media Report (2012).

References

Arab Knowledge Report (2009). *Towards productive intercommunication for knowledge.* Mohammed bin Rashid Al Maktoum Foundation. Available at: <http://www.arab-hdr.org/akr/AKR2009/English/AKR2009-Eng-Full-Report.pdf>.

Arab Social Media Report (2012). Socialmedia in the Arab world: Influencing societal and cultural change? *2*(1), 1−29. Available at: <http://www.arabsocialmediareport.com/UserManagement/PDF/ASMR%204%20updated%2029%2008%2012.pdf>.

Chappelle, C. A. (2010). Social media and the changing face of rationalist dissent in Iran: Lessons from the 2009 presidential election. Thesis submitted by the Webster Graduate School, London, of Webster University, St Louis, MO, in partial fulfilment of the requirements for the Degree of Master of Arts in International Relations.

Chorev, H. (2011). Social media and other revolutions. *Tel Aviv Notes, 5.* (19). Available at: <http://www.tau.ac.il/dayancenter/pdfim/TA_Notes_H_Chorev_Social_Media_101011.pdf>.

Comninos, A. (2011). *Twitter revolutions and cyber crackdowns: User-generated content and social networking in the Arab spring and beyond.* Association for Progressive Communications (APC). June.

Ghannam, J. (2011). *Social media in the Arab World: Leading up to the uprisings of 2011.* Report to the Center for International Media Assistance, 3 February. Available at: <http://cima.ned.org/sites/default/files/CIMA-Arab_Social_Media-Report%20-%2010-25-11.pdf>.

Jamali, R., & Abedin, B. (2013). Effects of family functions and structural changes on family business development (social capital evidence). *International Journal of Entrepreneurship and Small Business, 18*(1), 79−89.

Martin, C. (2011). An information literacy perspective on learning and new media. *On the Horizon, 19*(4), 268−275.

Moaddel, M. (2012). *The Arab spring and Egyptian revolution makers: Predictors of participation,* Population Studies Center Research Report 12-775, September. Ypsilanti, MI: Eastern Michigan University. Available at: <http://www.psc.isr.umich.edu/pubs/pdf/rr12-775.pdf>.

Narayan, D., & Cassidy, M. F. (2001). A dimensional approach to measuring social capital: Development and validation of a social capital inventory. *Current Sociology, 49*(2), 59−102.

Nijboer, J., & Hammelburg, E. (2010). Extending media literacy: A new direction for libraries. *New Library World, 111*(1/2), 36−45.

Price, M. (2012). Iran and the soft war. *International Journal of Communication, 6,* 2397−2415.

Serag, Y. M. (2011). *From social networking to political and physical impacts: Some lessons from the Egyptian lotus revolution.* Available at: <http://www.regionalstudies.org/uploads/conferences/presentations/international-conference-2011/serag.pdf>.

Further reading

Nye, J. S. (2004). *Soft power: The means to success in world politics.* New York, NY: Public Affairs.

Putnam, R. D. (1993). The prosperous community: Social capital and public life. *American Prospect, 13,* 35−42.

Vuving, A. L. (2009). *How soft power works.* Paper presented at the panel 'Soft Power and Smart Power', Annual Meeting of the American Political Science Association, Toronto, 3 September.

National identity, crises of legitimacy and penetration of social networks

2

Socialisation and national identity

Imagine an infant. You know, that infant will need to go through the process of socialisation by way of interacting with the real world and the surrounding community. In the past, family and peers had the main role in this process. Nowadays, however, the mass media, with their permanent infusion of messages, play an undeniable role in the process as well, with many researchers believing the intensity of this role shapes the personal and social identity of individuals. However, things are different when the mass media are transformed into social media and personal identity is affected by these transformations. A study of 253 Iranians (between the ages of 18 and 32) who were not members of any social networks and 308 individuals who use social networks frequently presented interesting results. Simple statistical analysis of the participants showed significant differences in national identity scores in that the first group scored 4.37 and the second group scored 3.32 (out of 7). In this regard, social networks act in two ways. First, encountering different ideas and beliefs and the gradual process of developing group attitudes attenuates the sense of national identity. Second, we may assume that individuals with weaker ties to their national identity will have a stronger tendency to join virtual social networks and consume mass media. A test was devised for this hypothesis, which showed that there were no significant differences between participants with a strong sense of national identity and those with a weak sense of national identity who had never joined an online social network, regarding their desire to join such a network.[1] To obtain more accurate results another test was conducted over a nine-month period. The national identity scores of 35 females and males who were not members of a social network were measured. The participants were asked to sign up to Facebook and spend at least three hours per week on the website. (That the participants met the minimum online time requirement was checked by the author.) The national identity scores of the participants was measured again after nine months. Except for a normal increase in three cases and nine cases where there was no change, there was significant decrease in the other participants' scores. In general, statistical analysis showed a significant change in national identity scores before and after use of the social networks. One probable explanation is that the author's sample faced a huge range of new ideas and opinions that affected the overall results. However, some national identity indices remained unchanged even among those showing a decreased score. Time restrictions prevented the conducting of further studies to see whether these indices would remain unchanged over a longer period, bearing in mind that the extent of variation of the indices depends on other factors, such as the period of membership of the social network. In the case of the Iranian members of social networks, for instance, one probable factor is that they might encounter a new sense of freedom, in contrast with members of more liberal societies where a social network may be taken for granted and not appear to be much of an extra freedom.

More studies are required for cases like Iran. Our results, for cases like Iran, arouse new concerns for government officials. They might ponder their dilemma: imposing limits on access to social networks raises worries about freedoms, democracy and human rights on one hand, while free access to social networks threatens national identity and widens the gap between the government and the nation, which may give rise to popular public movements in the long term. Different states adopt different policies when faced with such a dilemma. As mentioned briefly in the last chapter, there are other factors, such as a crisis of legitimacy, that may result in public movements. States that impose limitations on access to social networks must keep in mind that their priority should be meeting the expectations and needs of their people. It is clear, when one delves into the triggering factors of the recent Arabic revolutions, for example in the case of Egypt, that achieving national development, fighting corrupt administrative systems and seeking justice and welfare for all social classes are the most important motivators for social movements (Serag, 2011). These factors may increase a legitimacy crisis. Let us go further and assume that if Mohammad Bouazizi in Tunisia (the young man who set himself on fire) knew about the power of social networks, would he have made the same decision and sacrificed his own life? There are examples where social media, along with government corruption, may topple the regime.

What was interesting in that situation was that the mass media and journalists tried not to cover the news about the self-immolation of Mohammed Buazizi and even YouTube was filtered by the Tunisian government. Nevertheless, Facebook was the most important medium to inform the public in Tunisia and other countries (Comninos, 2011). This shows that protesters always find a way to express themselves in spite of all the precautions taken by the ruling power to control the situation. One of the main factors under consideration that could be the trigger for a legitimacy crisis is placing limitations on free political and social participation. Figure 2.1 illustrates the status of six countries regarding two questions: 'To what extent do you believe that lack of social and political participation increased your activities on social media?' The average is based on a seven-point scale (1 very low and 7 very high).

The term 'social participation' refers to individuals' concerns and engagement regarding social and personal responsibilities. It has been pointed out by many researchers that a falling rate of social participation may annihilate a regime or render a social life lacking in motivation. These are people who feel no control over their lives. Analysis of survey results in the five countries under consideration in the Middle East showed above average effectiveness of this factor. However, in the cases of Yemen and Jordan, the score obtained was far lower than those obtained in the other countries; in general, the scores obtained showed that social networks are a place to experience more social participation. On this platform, people who could not elect those in authority were entering virtual groups with which they shared

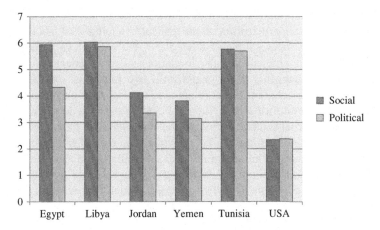

Figure 2.1 Effect of social and political participation on activity in social media.

common beliefs. They created their own group, managed it and felt responsible for other members within the group. They were free to share ideas and felt support, for example through the number of 'likes' they received via the social network Facebook. In the absence of any social participation in the real society, protesting virtually against the ruling power is not the only reason to join social networks, for there are feelings such as being effective to take into consideration. A brief comparison between the countries under study and the USA clarifies the results further. Prohibition of participation in social and political activities cannot be the reason for the tendency to use social networks in America. There are two possible explanations then: either the social and political participation of Americans in real society is higher than in the countries studied, or there must be a missing factor that explains this lower rate of participation (and the resulting effect of social and political participation on activities in the social media) among Americans.

The data from the next part of the questionnaire were used to examine the current level of political and social participation in real society. To see the results reverse Figure 2.1. The level of political and social participation among American individuals is in the range 3.54 to 3.91 compared with 2.05 to 2.8 for the five Arab countries. Although the position of the USA in the scale is not significantly high, it is acceptable. Thus the absence of individual participation in social and political activities will increase participation in social networks and the USA is no exception – American citizens may rush to social networks if they are banned from social and political activities. Another aspect of participation is known as *political participation*. This may emerge in the form of elections and supervision, in its direct form or participation and activity in political parties, in its indirect form. Clearly, the rate of participation depends on socio-economic level and quality of education. What is under scrutiny here is the general satisfaction of the public regarding its own political participation. Figure 2.1 shows the equal effect of social and political participation on the tendency to join social media. (Egypt is an exception, with these two forms of participation differing considerably.) The story is the same: the higher the level of participation in political activities in real life (as in the USA) the less effective the lack of political participation on the tendency to join social media.

The next factor that causes a legitimacy crisis is the surge in expectations of the public towards the government and the limitations of government in meeting the response. When this happens, social media fulfil two functions. On the one hand, people who feel that elected officials are not able to meet their expectations tend to join social networks and media in the hope of finding others who share their ideas and, consequently, groups that exaggerate the incapacity of their governors will arise. On the other hand, we have to keep in mind the role of information sharing and making people aware of information via social media. Members of social media networks have an increased opportunity to learn more about the good things other countries have achieved within a stable democracy, which further raises the level of expectation in those in less democratic countries. Evidently, people in the Middle East think that everything in the West is just perfect and that the West is heaven. Regardless of how much they hear about the challenges of the current economic crisis in the West, the image they have created is beyond question. Even if states in the Middle East manage to keep the status quo, social media raise demands and therefore the gap between what government can do and pubic expectation grows wider. The development of such groups in social networks that expose the weakness of governments in the Middle East will increase the legitimacy crisis and result in public movement.

Another factor in the legitimacy crisis is the failure to attract talent, that is, intellectuals and knowledgeable groups of citizens. Regimes that come to power thorough whatever means, but not the will of the people, try to attract as many of those who would go along with the ideas of the regime as possible. Talented individuals are reluctant to participate in public works in cooperation with such governments. This leads them to to set themselves apart, giving space to the incompetent. Just imagine how many groups were formed to prove the incapability of a ministry or even of a president in the countries of the Middle East after the expansion of the social media and how many cases resulted in resignation or dismissal, just to abate the pressure. These are all signals of weakness that increase the legitimacy crisis. To measure the probability of public movement in your country, observe your friends and acquaintances and ask them: 'What do you think about the regime? Is there any legitimacy for their governance?' Positive and negative answers say a lot about the situation.

Dimensions of national identity

In this section we look at several indices of national identity. To find a relation between participation in social media and national identity, the answers were categorised into two groups: 'high national identity' and 'low national identity'. Afterwards, the rate of participation in activities for the two groups was measured in two classes: 'political activities in the media' and 'cultural works and friendship connections'. Scores obtained for these two classes were compared between the two groups. Moreover, a correlation test was conducted to determine the relationship between national identity and rate of political activities in the media. To ensure reliable results, Keillor and Hult's questionnaire, with 90 citations at the time of the study, was employed to measure the national identity level (Keillor and Hult, 1999). Thus the validity of the scale is maintained. The reader must bear in mind that the scores obtained are for individuals who actively participate in social networks, and the author has no access to individuals who do not have an account in a social network. As mentioned, in Iran, for instance, the level of national identity of those in social networks is significantly lower than those without access to Facebook, Twitter and other social networks. The questionnaire comprised four main dimensions; each will be discussed.

National heritage

The first dimension – national heritage – measures how proud participants are of the history of their country (see Figure 2.2). When an individual signs up to a social network they gradually encounter new ideas and symbols which the youth in particular are more interested in and which overshadow patriotic attitudes. In spite of the rich history and civilisation of almost all the countries in the Middle East, the highest score for national heritage is surprisingly 3.43, for Egypt and Yemen (close to the average point). This score for the USA, with far less historical background is 4.09.

These statistics, however, only shed light on those interested in the political condition of the country, so we need to bring in new variables. First is the rate of participation in social networks as a place for political activities. Statistical analyses showed that the only case of an inverse relation between national heritage and political activities in the media is Tunisia. In other words, in Tunisia, a reduced sense of national heritage results in an increased tendency towards political activities in the

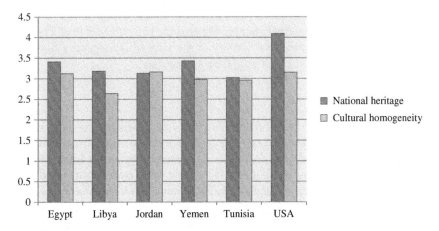

Figure 2.2 The level of NH and CH dimensions of national identity.

media. In brief, this result obtained only for Tunisia and in general no significant relationship was found between the variables, even regarding 'cultural works and friendship connections'.

Cultural homogeneity

Another aspect of national identity is cultural homogeneity, or a sense of pride in one's culture, nationality and common background with fellow citizens. The participants were asked about their feelings towards attending group work that, in some way, has to do with the improvement of their country. The reasonable assumption is that monoculture countries will enjoy higher scores in respect of this variable. However, the fact is, as illustrated in Figure 2.2, a country like the USA, with plenty of subcultures, has almost the same score as smaller (by population) Arabic countries. One explanation may be the role of the media, that promote one culture and encourage migrant groups to follow the ruling culture. Interesting results were found regarding the inverse relationship between cultural homogeneity and the tendency to join in political activities through social media (a lower cultural homogeneity score increases the tendency for political activity in the social media). This relationship does not only apply to the USA. Indeed, Americans at any level of score regarding the first two dimensions of national identity (national heritage and cultural homogeneity) have a greater tendency to participate in cultural work and enjoy connections with friends. It is interesting that, in spite of protests against the federal government in the last couple of years in the USA, development of communication still keeps its position compared with other variables such as political activities. One question bearing on cultural homogeneity is whether 'people frequently engage in activities that identify them as a "nation".' This question scored much lower than other questions in Arabic countries and contributed to a lower cultural homogeneity score in those countries. To confirm other results, another question was asked: 'To what extent do you participate in political groups supporting revision in government policies?' Indeed, the inclination to engage in political activities via social media was measured in a previous section and here we ask about the status quo of such activities. Again, except for the USA and Yemen, we found a significant relationship between the two variables in all countries, which means that a lower national identity in the cultural homogeneity dimension may result in higher political activities in the social media.

Belief system

The third dimension − the belief system − focuses on beliefs and religious orientations and attitudes, so that to some extent it deals with religious identity. Arabic countries in the Middle East and North Africa are characterised by strong Islamic ties and Arabic is known as the companion of Islam the whole world over. It is therefore worth looking more closely at Arab countries, bearing in mind that religion is deeply rooted in the countries included in the author's study. Where religion − as traditional principle − meets the media − as a modern toolset − we may expect considerable effects. As a set of tools, they hold great promise for the promotion of religious beliefs, as much as they can be a threat to those very beliefs. Iran was one of the successful countries, led by an insightful leader, to notice the role of the media in the development of country and religion. Ayatollah Khomeini mentioned in his speech in the early days after the Iranian revolution, 'Radio and television are nationwide public universities'.[2] Following this idea, nowadays the Iranian Broadcast Channel has become a strong tool for promoting religion. However, the media function well while there is no rival. Along with the development of satellite channels and access to the Internet among Iranian youth and religious campaigns by other countries, officials of Iranian state-run broadcasting have come to believe that a religious media war is being waged and have launched several websites to fight in that war. One of the more successful websites in this field is that of the Iranian Supreme Leader Ayatollah Khamenei,[3] which has a good record in drawing young people's attention. However, we are at the dawn of a new era of social media and religious officials are doing their best to produce material in the media to keep up with the pace of developments. Consider the situation in which the religious officials of a country are at war with groups mobilised all around the world to fight for their religious beliefs. Of course, there is no balance of power between the two parties in the fight. The question to ask then is: 'Is there any difference between the religious orientation of members and non-members of social networks?' As mentioned before, a study conducted among young members and non-members of social networks showed significant differences between the two groups, with the non-members scoring higher with regard to religious beliefs. An interesting point in the study was that members of social network groups held that religious beliefs must be demonstrated by performing good deeds and that doing religious rituals does not count. To put it in another way, being Muslim does not entail the need to perform certain religious rituals; rather what it does mean is to not commit any act which contradicts the religious training that one has received. However, members of certain social networks state that using the network to promote ideas that are pertinent to religious ethics is common practice. The participants feel a greater inclination to join groups with religious objectives. At the other end of the spectrum, non-member participants hold and perform certain religious rituals as one of the main signs of piety. It is noticeable that while these results may appear to generalise Arabic countries and do not take into account recent public movements, including those mentioned in the previous chapter, many have suddenly rushed to join social networks. Thus they might hold ideas close to those of non-member individuals. Yet what needs to be understood is that protesting against tyranny and fighting for freedom from dictators is pivotal in Islamic training, as is emphasised in recent public movements.

We will now consider the comparative survey of 'belief systems' in the countries under study (see Figure 2.3). All Arabic countries received a score above 4, except Yemen with 3.98, though this is still considerably higher than average. This is not surprising, considering the relatively strong religious philosophy in that region, binding the individual with their nationality − no one denies their religious beliefs.

In addition, the score for the question regarding religious activities appears too high, which hints that such activities are the medium for interactive groups, whether for religious or other purposes. As Figure 2.3 shows, the USA scored lower than the five Arabic countries, for which the multicultural population of the country is

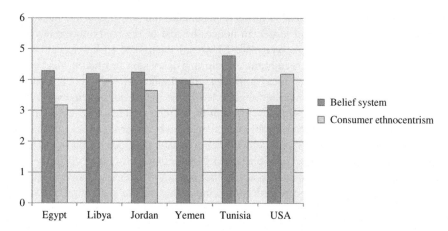

Figure 2.3 The level of BS and CE dimensions of national identity.

to blame. We also found that people with higher belief systems scores tend to join religious groups and avoid political groups. In summary, the results imply that Islam was and still is one of the strongest ties in these communities, even after the development of the cyberworld. Even respondents with low levels of religious belief admit the important role of religion in their activities. To find out more about the current position of Islam in these countries, respondents were asked: 'To what extent do you think that the current ruler is in harmony with your religious standards?' All countries except Egypt (3.21) scored less than 3, which corresponded with the dissatisfaction of the respondents in this regard. Should religious concerns be one of the factors of a public movement, we may expect other movements in the near future, unless groups with a high belief-system score are satisfied.

The last question in the questionnaire that helps us with role of religion is: 'Have you ever tried to share your viewpoints in social networks concerning the following issues?' As evidenced in Table 2.1, religious and internal policies are the main concerns of members of social networks, while external and foreign policy is of least concern. Other important concerns are corruption in the public sector and culture. This hints at the movement of religious activities from the real world to the cyberworld, as it is one of the integral concerns of humankind. As mentioned in the case of Iran, such activities may differ in nature from actual religious activities, as the cyberworld features the introduction of so-called intellectual and liberal thinking, so that while the notion of religious activities has not changed, to some extent their nature is different.

Consumer ethnocentrism

The last aspect under consideration is 'consumer ethnocentrism', which refers to how consumers prefer home-made products. It is worth pointing out Ayatollah Khamenie's insightful decision to name 2012 as 'the year of national production' in Iran. For one thing, economic sanctions imposed on Iran have empowered national production and

Table 2.1 **Rate of social network usage (%)**

	Culture	Corruption in public sector	Religion	External and foreign policy	Internal policy
Egypt	41	57	58	31	51
Libya	37	61	57	37	56
Jordan	48	36	61	21	44
Yemen	41	35	65	26	52
Tunisia	42	46	62	37	52
USA	34	22	31	27	42

for another, more emphasis is placed on national identity. Of course, the best policy to lessen the negative effects of sanctions for an import-based economy is to scale down the import of raw materials and to support exports, in order to increase national revenue. The indices of consumer ethnocentrism thus demonstrate the opportunity for government measures aimed at success. The development of social media is coincident with changes in public purchasing attitudes. Cherishing consumerism is commonly observed, as marketing is an intrinsic function of social media, if changing the lifestyle and purchasing behaviour in favour of international corporations is not their first priority. First, we dealt with the data from Iran and found a significant difference between consumer ethnocentrism in member and non-member groups. The former scored an average of 3.11, with 3.93 for the latter. Changes in the national identity of individuals in social media are undeniable. As shown in Figure 2.3, while the USA scored 4.19, all the Arabic countries scored less than 4. Further study of the relationship between this aspect and respondents' behaviour showed an inverse relation between consumer ethnocentrism and engaging in political activities, except in the USA. A lower score on this dimension is accompanied by a higher inclination to engage in political activities and to comment on internal policy issues. Moreover, political groups supporting change in government policies are more attractive to this group. All these tell us that national products lose their markets to foreign products, along with a rise in anti-government movements. One explanation is that government is the first to be blamed for the poor quality of national products and industries. This is more evident in the mainly state-run economies in the Middle East, where people tend to blame the government for every problem, even if the government has nothing to do with it. It looks essential for governments, therefore, to promote national products, as did the Iranian government in 2012.

Notes

1. The test was conducted only for Iran as the data on non-member individuals actively using social media in Arabic countries were not available.
2. http://farsi.khamenei.ir/imam-content?id=9696
3. http://khamenei.ir

References

Comninos, A. (2011). *Twitter revolutions and cyber crackdowns: User-generated content and social networking in the Arab spring and beyond.* Association for Progressive Communications (APC), June.

Keillor, B. D., & Hult, G. T. M. (1999). A five-country study of national identity Implications for international marketing research and practice. *International Marketing Review, 16*(1), 65−82.

Serag, Y. M. (2011). *From social networking to political and physical impacts: Some lessons from the Egyptian lotus revolution.* Available at: http://www.regionalstudies.org/uploads/conferences/presentations/international-conference-2011/serag.pdf.

Social media and social capital (with an emphasis on security) 3

Security and social capital

Some researchers maintain that social capital means 'goodwill' between people and within groups, and includes further sub-categories such as 'social awareness, self-management, trust, and so on' (McCallum and O'Connell, 2009). Suppose you live in a society in which you have no power over social life and the government. Such a way of life induces the feeling that a greater power is working to manipulate social life and is trying to strengthen its grip on every aspect. How secure might you feel living in such a society? There is a mutual relationship between the terms 'security' and 'social capital'. A sense of trust grows in a society when the people feel healthy mentally, secure economically and free to make decisions. Moreover, a sense of trust improves security, which in this chapter is considered a prerequisite of social capital. A questionnaire designed by the author was used to evaluate the security of the society in the countries under study. Although other studies used economic factors as the main indicator of the security of a society, this study deals only with:

(i) the role of political factors in social security;
(ii) factors in individual decision-making at the national level;
(iii) people's participation in the security of society; and
(iv) the actual extent of the rule of law. The questionnaire comprised 27 questions.

The role of political factors in social security

This section deals with the role fulfilled by the power of political parties, their freedom, their role in national development, and the intensity of control and supervision of the parties. Indeed, people perceive trust in strong parties as a mediator between themselves and the government. They find parties to be reliable tools through which they can supervise the political affairs of their society. Social security in this regard was evaluated in Egypt and the results showed people were strongly dependent on political parties and found them effective factors in planning their future. The recent revolution in Egypt and relative freedoms afterward resulted in the sudden emergence and multiplication of political parties. On the one hand this gave the people of the country a chance to join at least one party, and on the other seriously violated trust in the parties. In fact, Egyptians trusted only the three political parties from the former regime, rather than the many parties that had recently emerged, a phenomenon that has affected the solidarity of the nation.

Online Arab Spring.

This ubiquitous mistrust is evident even in the mass media, so that a surge of posts for or against specific political parties has taken place. This plurality of political parties cannot be found in Libya, Jordan, Yemen and Tunisia. The parties active in these countries are exactly those that would have been active in the pre-revolution era. The Egyptian people have experienced a loss of their sense of belonging, while inter-group trust has grown. This is a serious threat in Egypt, as well as in the other four countries mentioned above, to a lesser extent. In such a situation, people try to show off their own talents instead of emphasising the role of the group. This leads to individualism in society. We must remember that a party is a political unit comprised of a group of citizens, and aims to play a more profound role in the lives of the citizens by defeating other parties. Thus, by building intra-group trust, social capital results in more powerful parties. To be clearer, let's draw an analogy between political parties and domestic businesses: just as a business with more customers than its competitors outperforms those competitors in term of profitability and social standing, so those parties with more members enjoy more power. Thus political parties adopt marketing approaches with an emphasis on concepts such as social responsibility, an idea known in the business world as *corporate social responsibility* (CSR). As found in the literature, the social responsibility of businesses is defined as a commitment to dedicate a portion of their income to non-profit and charity works (Lichtenstein, Drumwright, & Braig, 2004). In other words, the basic idea of CSR is to be responsive to the legitimate expectations of stakeholders (Nijhof, de Bruijn, & Honders, 2008). A wide range of customers, citizens, employees and so on constitutes the stakeholders. A notable point that is also of concern in the present text is that people from different cultures and different nationalities have different perceptions of the responsiveness of the multinationals (Endacott, 2003). Therefore, although it is rarely achieved, having an identical influence on all the members of the party (who might be from different countries) is very fruitful. One of the best ways to lure or even trick customers into visiting a firm's web page is to emphasise popular social responsibility. That is, a better choice of social responsibility is not necessarily one that is of more benefit for the society, but rather the more popular the social responsibility the better. This leads less popular firms to copy the social responsibility strategy of competitors, a phenomenon known as *social responsibility mimicry*. Other authors believe that the Internet can be a means to collect information on and feedback from the stakeholders (Branco and Rodrigues, 2008). This highlights another aspect of companies' social responsibility, which indicates that a specific social responsibility strategy can be designed for specific groups of people. To this end, the Internet and social networks are the best means. Following this strategy, political parties try to attract groups of people, who may join the party for reasons very different from those of other members. Suppose a party tries to convey the idea that it will pursue more social freedom for women and more effective child labour laws if the party wins an upcoming election. Clearly, propagating this message in social networks is highly effective in attracting more followers. But the question is whether there is any relationship between the extent of social responsibility and the support received from the social media. The first measure of social capital is 'group characteristics' which encompass issues such as the number of members and their participation in decision-making. Group characteristics have a two-sided effect: on the one hand the party tries to attract more members, while on the other hand people tend to join larger groups with more power to influence social matters. Furthermore, it is clear that the higher the number of members in a group, the less the influence held by a single member. However, effectiveness and participation in group decisions, within the realm of social media, are no longer a concern and people only want to be a member of the group, even if they play no role in that group. Social interactions are the fundamental elements of any society. From a network viewpoint, relations and ties are taken as social capital, through which people enjoy accessing the resources and support available in the network. As noted, however, as in physical society, the individual gradually loses their chance to have a say in group decision-making. The most notable issue regarding symbols of technology in Arabic countries is that the Internet, for example, is dealt with as a problem. Consequently, its development and expansion has been problematic and not surprisingly the main functions of the Internet and social media have been introduced into these countries only after a delay of some years. In the early days of the introduction of the Internet into a society, entertainment functions overshadow its other uses. This explains why the positive functions of the Internet, such as higher participation rates and civic engagement, lag behind, although these are *per se* subject to mediatory factors, such as trusting the websites, the development of communication infrastructures, political development and demographic variables.

Factors in individual decision-making at the national level

Among the different roles of social media as accelerators of revolution in Arabic countries, participation stands out absolutely. Our survey of the four Arabic countries revealed that an increase in public participation was the main factor in the expansion of the media in society and in this regard 'participation training' was most effective. Doubtless, social media have a profound effect on increasing/decreasing participation in social issues and social phenomena. They fulfil a leading role by motivating, supporting and informing groups of people and uncovering social matters. Thus social media can lead and organise public participation or grab public attention on a specific social issue – an invitation to participate in or boycott an election is one common example. For instance, the activists and users of social media in Iran were the same in the two presidential elections of 2009 and 2013; however, in the former case they played a destructive role, while in the latter they constructively spread hope nationwide. Although the activists in the social media in Iran played a different role by opposing the presidency of Dr Ahmadi Nejad in 2009 and supporting Dr Rouhani in 2013, they played a notable role in increasing participation and demonstrating the extent of social capital in Iran. Participation, *per se*, needs 'knowledge', which is transferred by training. Therefore, by providing that training, the social media play a notable role in the development of social capital.

It is noticeable that such training is not provided as an integrated and organised programme, but instead happens through a wide variety of posts by the users. That is, there is no recognisable body that undertakes training in social media but rather all users play an active role in mutual learning; this learning is based on trust in the wisdom of the crowd. Training by the mass media can be misleading as it can be manipulated by the parties to meet their specific political wills, which is quite different from the general perception of training. Training is the fundamental and vital goal of social activities and development in different fields depends on it. Nowadays, political parties put emphasis on providing training opportunities for the users of social media from different social classes. Attention to and expectations from training are growing in parallel, so that where once it was enough to hold a training course and find enough participants, now parties also expect the training to facilitate their political goals. Thus parties' training activity in the social media is concerned with both providing the training and ensuring the effectiveness of such training.

Behavioural learning theory (that the individual learns through personal experience) partly explains the learning mechanism; however, it fails to elaborate and justify the whole learning process in its more complicated and wider context. The social learning theory, therefore, states that in addition to direct experience, learning may occur by observing others' actions and outcomes. In other words, as the theory implies, learning is the outcome of mutual and continuous interactions and influences between the individual and the social environment, and these influences are amplified by the social media. That is, behavioural changes (as a result of learning) depend on:

- whether what is taught is important for the learner;
- whether what is taught is found useful by the learner;
- whether what is taught is found practical by the learner.

The answer to all these questions is 'yes', given that there is great variety in the subjects of training and individuals can choose what they learn. However, the intention of political parties is not academic training, but rather the manipulation of political training to attract more people. The role of the social media in introducing parties and politicians to the countries studied in this book, which are characterised by social relations based mostly on oral culture, has been to document this oral culture and to improve public awareness, so that liberal thoughts are probably the outstanding feature of this awareness. Political training and the propagation of information by political parties, of course, are in line with the goals and plans of the parties. To gain public support and trust political parties always have to support national interests and goals, while at the same time following their own strategies, especially during elections. To be effective bodies in the political awareness of the public, parties have to acquire the trust of the people. Political parties need to gain public support and in order to do so elaborate and justify their ideologies and programmes.

Transforming public culture into political culture is another function of the social media in Arabic countries. There is a direct relationship between training in political culture and participation in civic society. Not surprisingly, a society which is poor in political culture is more eager to find access to training sources and join social media. A critical element of the political behaviour and actions of people in a society is their political culture, as it may influence people — political actors — by indirectly imposing values and models. On account of the variety of factors in the formation of political culture throughout the ages, including geographical region and political system, studying political culture is not straightforward. It is a function of public culture and this relationship between the two is evident in every society. The difference between political culture and public culture is the former's focus on the structure and function of power and authority, whether practically or fundamentally. Indeed, the basic rules of implementing policies are determined by political culture, which also dictates the common beliefs and thoughts that constitute the foundations of political life. The different behaviours of nations in the political field can be explained by studying the political cultures of those nations. The functions of any state are based on a social ground making the political culture essential for retaining power and sovereignty; thus the state manipulates the political culture to guarantee its survival. This means that coordination between the political culture and the political system will lead to political stability. In general, political culture consists of political attitudes, knowledge and skills. In fact, by studying people's attitudes toward the political system we can learn about the political culture of a society. Political culture is a measure of knowledge about power and politics within different social classes. For example, one feature of the political culture in underdeveloped societies — and even in some Arabic countries, such as Jordan and Yemen — is an indifference to political matters, while other countries, such as Egypt, are far more developed in this regard. Indeed, the development of the political culture aided by the social media played a notable role in the outbreak of the recent revolution in Egypt. In the light of this, the authorities in Iran and Saudi Arabia felt it necessary to implement Internet filtering programs to attenuate the role of social media in the public domain. Through such filtering, they tried to stop the development of the political culture, and it is illuminating that this was done under the pretext of religious concerns. Indeed, the authorities have never admitted to the political concerns behind the filtering programs. A notable point regarding the role of social media in the development of political culture is that the mass media in the majority of Middle Eastern countries are state-run. As a result, these media broadcast only pro-government messages, prompting people to turn toward social media to access real information. Government-imposed limitations have resulted in the building of trust in the social media and political parties have made the best use of such trust. The mass media mediate between the people and their environment and usually transfer concepts that have been manipulated, through multilateral interactions, by groups and individuals. On the other hand, instead of mediating, social media are part of the environment and their most outstanding feature is their continuous evolution. At the same time, the extent to which political culture is transferred changes so that the culture can be manipulated by a new power at any moment. The fact is that while powerful media alone are quite capable of triggering big changes in public opinion, their power lies in their ability to empower specific modes of thought so that they create public readiness for change, or they may even go further and steer that change.

There are many factors in this readiness, a crisis that attacks public belief in the rul-ing system. When this happens, individuals with weaker group ties tend to be more open to hear what the opposition has to say. Thus it is not surprising to see a surge of desire for change when social stability and group solidarity (social capital) begin to decline. When this happens, the mass media have more power to trigger new ideas in the society, or at least a popular character can grab the opportunity and reach out to the public. Indeed, the infusion of information by the social media is so immense that people in contact with these media are inevitability informed about develop-ments and share their findings with others. All these trends and factors, although ambiguous and intangible, influence our behaviour, although the trend is so slow and so shallow that it cannot be taken as direct suggestion. For instance, in some developing countries, including Iran and other Arabic countries, state TV and radio channels, intentionally or unintentionally, follow the Western style of propagating a culture of consumption and in general advertise a life of routine, stagnated social structure and underdevelopment. These policies, somehow, pave the way for a cul-tural invasion. In fact many policy-makers in third-world countries, whether inten-tionally or not, have adopted Western attitudes and propagate Western social institutions and values, regardless of their native cultures. In addition, as mentioned above, people in these countries are deeply influenced by this trend even though they do not trust the state media. Bearing this in mind, imagine how effective the social media can be in influencing the public culture, given the trust people have in these media. A comparison was conducted between the level of public trust in mass and social media (Figure 3.1).

As Figure 3.1 shows, there is a notable difference between the levels of trust in the mass media and in the social media in Arabic countries, which is not compara-ble with that in the USA. The fact that many of the mass media in the USA are run by the private sector, whereas the government controls the mass media in Arabic countries, is one of the reasons for this difference. It is noticeable that extended

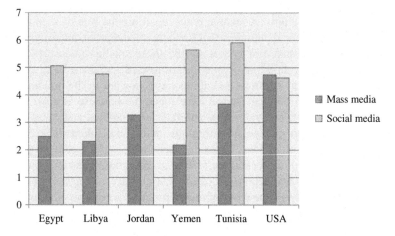

Figure 3.1 Level of trust in the news from mass media and social media.

control by the state of the mass media and censorship imposed on the news lead many to look for accurate and complete news items in the social media. The media relies on public trust for survival and thus it is not surprising that many mass media organisations in Arabic countries do not survive long. Therefore the rebuilding of public trust is one of the first priorities of state-run media in these countries.

Factors in participation in the security of society

Although the security of society is one of the tasks of government, it is not achievable without public participation. Such participation is crucial for establishing social security and specific methods must be adopted to internalise it. A key factor in participation is awareness, as nationalistic attitudes grow when people are informed about national issues. An individual cannot be expected to be interested in a matter of which they do not have any knowledge. Threats and risky situations, even if not based on solid facts, induce awareness. All living creatures naturally tend to react to threats. Lack of security in a society is an immense threat, which is sometimes neglected by the people owing to lack of awareness of the problem, which in turn presents another threat to the society. Awareness of threats and dangers can also be approached from a psychological point of view, addressing how to inform people about the lack of security. For instance, the social media in Iran have introduced a destructive phenomenon that threatens the security of the society. Now the question is: how can people accept the social media as a threat when they do not trust the source that propagates that idea? Thus the loss of trust in one type of media and the build-up of trust in another changes participation in social security, as people do not trust the media that call for public participation. Islam, in the countries under study, is a key player. The Islamic order 'to enjoin good and prohibit evil' resembles active public participation in the society, which is called by sociologists 'social capital'. Reduction of social capital and public participation leave no other way for the government but to rely more on force. The mere utilisation of force makes many of those who are needed to actualise and implement the force leave the body of government, which in turn leads to the hard-line approach to security, putting more emphasis on threat. Moreover, as the government does not enjoy public support, approaches to security take over social dynamics and the main portion of expenditure.

The most basic pro-participation belief is an acknowledgement of the equality of citizens. The purpose is to improve cooperation, sharing and sympathy among individuals, which leads to a qualitative and quantitative improvement in life in economic, social and political fields. Participation is a process that people use to initiate change in their environment and themselves. These changes are frequently emphasised by Islam. Social participation necessarily needs the proper ground in which to evolve. Development of such proper ground depends on the empowerment of civic society, institutions and pertinent processes. In principle, the development of civic society entails the institutionalisation of common bodies and real public participation, in turn, leads to the empowerment of civic society. Features such as volunteerism, awareness and the desire to participate connect participation to civic society. Volunteer associations prepare individuals for social participation. Civic institutes include guild unions, political parties, private business groups, cooperatives, art associations, newspapers, charity organisations and even neighbourhood gatherings. Social media highlight the voluntary bases of these activities as no one can prohibit or dictate membership of a virtual association.

Therefore, as frequently emphasised by Islam, trust and participation are two key elements of social capital and, in this regard, the social media amplify participation. It is notable that God and fate are two undeniable factors in people's lives in the Arab countries of the Middle East and Iran and overshadow the notion of the individual will. While social media do not tackle this belief, they induce the idea that people can play a determining role in their lives. The social media do this by introducing man's will as a part of God's will in determining the fate of society and the people. In this way, improving self-belief is the smallest role played by social media in Arabic countries.

Actual extent of the rule of law

As the survey results revealed, there is a correlation between the actual extent of the rule of law and the two variables of social capital, trust and volunteerism. The greater the rule of law, the more interested people are in helping others, which in turn results in the growth of trust. Our results showed that for Arab people the actual rule of law is measured by two key factors:

- total number of people in society who are treated equally by the law;
- participation of people in legislation through free elections.

There is a wide gap between the gravity of these factors for the people and the actual status of society regarding these factors in the Arab countries. The interesting point is that the surveys were carried out after the revolutions and people were still dissatisfied regarding these two factors. The widest gap was observed in Egypt, with many Egyptians believing that the new constitution would actually increase injustice in society and grant more power to Mohammad Morsi. The fact that, under the new law, the authorities were granted immunity of jurisdiction was interpreted as an expansion of injustice in society. In the absence of social media, lack of social power leads to a sort of political strangulation in society, which gradually limits the power of the rule of law over the government. The social power of the people in Arabic countries re-emerged within the frame of virtual media after the introduction of social media, which enabled the flow of transparent information and criticism of the government's actions. The inequality of people before the law is not limited to discrimination against or in favour of some officials and authorities, but can be traced even to relatively small issues such as prohibiting women from driving cars in Saudi Arabia. Discrimination against women in Saudi Arabia has inspired several anti-government campaigns on Facebook which, like any critic of the government, has triggered worries among the leaders of the country. As mentioned in Chapter 1, along with the increasing participation in the elections of 2009 in Iran, social media have played a notable role in spreading the idea that election results could be manipulated. In this case, people found their right to decide their own future was in jeopardy. Participation in the legislative process is the dominant demonstration of people's sovereignty and right to determine their own political and social fate. People, nowadays, implement this right indirectly and through their representatives in parliament. However, the role that people can play in social media, i.e. supervision, is more crucial. Figure 3.1 demonstrates that lack of trust in the mass media is more evident than trust in the social media. Another way to approach this is to ask if there are any differences between participants in the social media and non-participants with regard to the level of social trust. In view of the problems in studying non-members in Arab countries, the first part of the study was limited to Iran. Interestingly, the results showed that no significant differences can be supported regarding these two groups. However, the participants in the two groups agreed on the fact that lack of trust in society, lack of knowledge of people's rights and social problems at the macro level, such as poverty, can be considerably effective in attracting more people to social media as a way to claim their legitimate rights.

In conclusion, the results of a study based on a theme analysis of 1,434 randomly selected tweets from five countries in 2013 are presented in Figure 3.2 (note that private messages, images and irrelevant tweets were removed from the analyses). Evidently cases '4' and '6' are highly pertinent to social security and social capital, topics covered in this chapter. Tweets (i.e. participation) in these two fields comprised 43 per cent of the tweets analysed in the study.

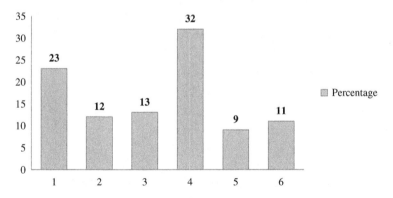

1 = Expanding freedom of expression
2 = Government's obligation to improve livelihoods
3 = Necessity of elections
4 = Developing social security through democracy
5 = Fighting government corruption, illegitimate rulers and taking corrupted rulers to court
6 = Equality before the law especially for authorities and rulers

Figure 3.2 Themes of non-private tweets in political fields in 2013.

References

Branco, M. C., & Rodrigues, L. L. (2008). Factors influencing social responsibility disclosure by Portuguese companies. *Journal of Business Ethics*, *83*(4), 685−701.

Endacott, R. W. J. (2003). Consumers and CRM: A national and global perspective. *Journal of Consumer Marketing*, *21*(3), 183−189.

Lichtenstein, D. R., Drumwright, M. E., & Braig, B. M. (2004). The effect of corporate social responsibility on customer donations to corporate-supported nonprofits. *Journal of Marketing*, *68*(4), 16−32.

McCallum, S., & O'Connell, D. (2009). Social capital and leadership development: Building stronger leadership through enhanced relational skills. *Leadership and Organization Development Journal*, *30*(2), 152−166.

Nijhof, A., de Bruijn, T., & Honders, H. (2008). Partnerships for corporate social responsibility: A review of concepts and strategic options. *Management Decision*, *46*(1), 152−167.

Effects of information and media literacy in social movements

The complexity of the media

Academic communities and universities are no longer the only places for the growth of knowledge as the mass media currently play an undeniable role in its development and propagation.

The mass media have stopped being the mere broadcasters of information and tend to be more selective of the information they focus on. For the mass media to be neutral, broadcasting whatever ideas are passed to them without prejudice, is an unrealistic proposition. For instance, if we consider television, its structure and nature, and the influence of its message, we can see that it is more than just an amplifier of sound and purveyor of images. Television is something more than a mere mediator and to understand this idea, and that of the complexity of the media, needs media literacy. The question is, what section of society in Arab countries is equipped with media literacy and understands the complexity of the media? While we discuss the power of the mass media in this book, it must be remembered that many people in Arab countries do not have access to these media and the Internet is not as yet the dominant medium in these countries. It must be borne in mind that the leaders of the recent revolutions were the youth, who have at least a minimum of information literacy; the source of Iran's revolution three decades ago, on the other hand, was the common people, the main body of society, who used traditional media such as the mosque for communication. The traditional media overtook the modern state-run media in Iran's revolution, while in the case of Arab countries it is the online media that have overtaken the traditional mass media, such as television and newspapers. Another point is the high rate of illiteracy among women in Arab countries, which suggests that women are not as able to lead the revolution as are men.

Information literacy is a step up they may be handed, from standard literacy. According to Wallis (2005), the term 'information literacy' covers the skills required to make use of and navigate in the electronic environment. The importance of information literacy is more evident when specific information is needed and the ability to find, evaluate and utilise that information is required. Such needs swelled at the peak of the public movements in Arab countries. People were relying mainly on the social media to find out about public demonstrations, gathering places and information about corrupt leaders. In addition, the people's inclination to lead the revolution and their need to find first-hand information were further reasons for the expansion of social media during the unrest. This need for information in Arab countries with rich oil resources has always been a challenge. While it is undeniable that information literacy in developed societies powers national growth, what about Arab countries? In spite of societies based on competitive economies in which people are rewarded based on their own work and success, in societies run on the income from oil, groups with more power and money receive a larger proportion of national income and rent. Clearly, bringing down one government and forming a new one is only a matter of replacing people and the system soon returns to its normal track – society, in other words, watches a new group of more rich and powerful people replace the old group. An outstanding feature of these societies is the deep doubts that are held regarding the powerful in society as people commonly believe that the rich and the powerful have reached their position not by their competency and work but rather because of their relationships with the new rulers – which is true in many cases. Consequently, information needs, even where information literacy exists, are directed to expand mistrust in the leaders. However, this does not lead to fundamental changes, as the built-up hatred targets individuals, not the whole system. Thus the movements for reform replace people rather than systems, giving rise to a vicious circle of underdevelopment in Arab countries. This phenomenon explains why two years after the revolutions in the Arab world, these countries still experience unrest, as there is always a group who oppose the leaders even when the system functions properly. A notable example of this is the huge campaign supporting the presidency of Mohammad Morsi, which at the time of writing, has turned into an 'anti-Morsi' campaign and he is currently on trial. Although information literacy appears to be highly developed in Arab countries, the image is a false one, and as post-revolution events show, a deep information illiteracy has expanded in society. A key factor in this illiteracy is the surge in users of social media, many joining these networks for the first time and only to find information. This widens the gap between real users and immediate users. The latter group can induce serious challenges ahead of the realisation of the actual goals of the revolution, as they make decisions based on their current emotions. They rush to participate in the revolution in the heat of their passion and forget the revolution as fast as they decided to join it in the first place. It is unreasonable to expect public recognition of concepts such as rationality, dialogue and so on, which are appropriate grounds for information literacy education. The pace of technology development is so high as to be unstoppable. There is no solution for the problem when it is too big. Thus Arab countries and others that took part in the recent outbreaks of revolution are not comparable with developed countries and the large numbers of social network users in the former does not mean high levels of information literacy. The key outcome of information literacy is the removal of limitations by means of which underdeveloped nations may be compensated for the damage they have sustained from colonising countries or their own corrupt leaders. This, unfortunately, is not the case in Arab countries – at least until now, though the future is not bright for them. Underdevelopment, together with the desire to develop, are good motivations for the outbreak of revolution, but a revolution which is led by an illiterate society again leads to underdevelopment. Iran's revolution is a good example for those believing that revolution leads to development. The question is whether Iranians have enjoyed more development since the recent revolution than they would have if revolution had taken place. This is not an easy question to answer. However, the growth of government and non-government corruption, emphasised by the recent expansion of mistrust in the government and the system, and the development of quantitative rather that qualitative science, all hint that the Iranian revolution has not been as successful as it is portrayed. Even the development of higher education and literacy in Iran is counterbalanced by a 'brain drain'. The revolution is therefore diverging from its original goals. To have a better picture, let's look at the statistics provided by a small-scale study in Mashhad and Tehran, with 1,362 participants:

- Among the respondents aged below 30, 58% believed Iran's revolution has failed to reach its goals; this figure for respondents above 30 is 36%. This age-based grouping was intended to create two groups: those who had experienced the revolution and those who had not. The difference between attitudes of the two groups is clear enough.
- In summary, among those who believed that the revolution has failed to meet its goals, 29% blamed the gap between society and the ruling system, 23% blamed the lack of specialist knowledge among the rulers and the authorities to enable proper decisions to be made, and 18% blamed the rulers' emphasis on short-term goals just to stay in power; the remaining participants blamed other causes. For a clear result, the information literacy of people at the time of revolution needs to be evaluated, which is not possible.

Literacy and political knowledge

At any rate, the outcome of literacy and social media in combination, which leads to the acceleration of revolution, is an increase in political knowledge. People can turn their potential power into actual power using political knowledge. People's power without political knowledge has no chance of mobilisation. Political knowledge paves the way for the actualisation of this power. The mass media in Arabic countries and Iran have always tried to keep the public unaware of what is going on in society by focusing on trivial matters. This gives more room to the rulers to drown in corruption. The emergence of social media in this situation jeopardises the tranquility of corrupt rulers – this is not a phenomenon unique to Arab and Middle East countries, as rulers in the USA have faced problems after the expansion of social media (e.g. WikiLeaks). Undoubtedly, then, expansion of social media affects the public trust in the ruling system. In other words, in spite of the mass media, the social media are part of the changes, rather than being reporters of the changes. Social media have proved their power during the outbreak of revolution in Arab countries, but now they have emerged as a factor that influences developments in society. Their effects began with the increase of political knowledge. Developments in Egypt showed that although a superficial peace can be ordered by imposing limitations on political-social space, such measures never stop the development of opposition in other forms and other spaces. The case of Egypt is an example whereby cutting mobile communication and Internet speed and filtering specific websites are all nothing but passive measures that cannot manage the movements. When Internet access is limited by the government, the first question people ask is, what could possibly have been on the Internet that made the government cut it? The limitation imposed increases the eagerness of the public to learn about what is going on in society via the Internet, which leads to the development of political knowledge. A common point regarding all the countries under study is the trend in human progress, which can be measured by the increase in the number of literate people and those receiving higher education. This trend leads to an increase in awareness and expectations. The increase in literacy in Iranian and Arab societies during the last 30 years is quite evident and it has coincided with the information and communication revolution that has increased access to information at the international level and familiarisation with people's way of life in other places. Development of the Internet, satellite TV and mobile phones has eliminated the traditional gaps between people in one country and those in another. The corruption of rulers can no longer be concealed from the public. As they learn about how developed countries are ruled and how people in these countries live, people in developing countries are asking why their rich natural resources (such as oil) do not bring them a minimum level of economic and social welfare, while their rulers have a luxurious lifestyle. Raising such questions in social media grabs the attention of other users and from there the attention of the general public. Any question that is frequently asked in the public mind and finds no reasonable answer can lead to revolution. It is evident then that the imposition of limitations on social media – a common practice in Iran, Saudi Arabia and even Bahrain – is the result of fear that questions will be asked and of the synergy of public power.

At any rate, the role of foreign actors and media in these public movements is undeniable. It is clear for those studying the Syrian crisis as a case in point that a number of social network pages are actually collecting information for intelligence purposes, rather than for the public sharing of that information, while foreign countries never miss any chance to add fuel to the flames. This specific interest in Syria is rooted in the fact that the country is one of the last hopes for the West to regain its lost power in the region. In this situation, the role of information literacy is emphasised by recognising the difference between reliable and fake news. Here, the new concept of 'media literacy' emerges, which is the ability to combine and analyse such information.

Information literacy education in developing countries

For the countries of the Middle East, information literacy education is absolutely critical. Under the permanent threat of Western powers' bringing down governments and taking control of natural resources, the Middle Eastern countries need, more than any others, to inform their people. Otherwise, the people in these countries are easily attracted to superficially intellectual and showy messages from the West with the aim of bringing down their governments. The main way to transfer the skills needed to use information and enable the citizen to live in the information society is information literacy education. The value of such education lies in the fact that a proper programme can be designed to be implemented in a proper way to achieve pre-set goals. In comparison with trial and error, which is prescribed by some to gain experience, the information education system is far more effective. In the absence of such education, people tend to waste a great deal of valuable energy and time, which is surely unacceptable in the competitive world of rapid change. Thus the first steps to information literacy education to be taken by the Middle East countries are as follows:

1. The information people expect from the government should be determined. That is, a lack of sufficient knowledge of government performance partially explains the outbreak of revolution. States tend to build a wall between themselves and their people, and this results in the growth of hatred and mistrust. The path towards development and respect is straighter when the people and their rulers trust each other. When such trust is built up, real participation emerges in the light of the common goals of the public and the rulers, coordination of forces and facilities, and cooperation among thinkers.

   When a society lacks this trust, people and groups dedicate part of their power and facilities to opposing each other, to removing misunderstanding, and to monitoring their rivals. Indeed, lack of trust between the people and the government is costly and valuable resources, which could have been used in the development of the country, are wasted on resolving this mistrust and tackling rival groups. One way to rebuild trust is to provide honest reports of the measures taken and the development of the political and international situation. Mistrust between the people and the state, in the face of the threat of foreign invasion, results in a serious loss of military power while the pace of national development is considerably slowed, or even stopped. Denying information about foreign contracts, censorship, concealing state corruption, providing coverage for the corrupt agents – all induce mistrust between the people and the state. Where there is national mistrust, dictatorship, oppression and mental anxiety grow faster, along with the spread of bad habits such as lying and flattery. What accelerated revolution in the Arab countries was that the rulers believed that their main wealth lay in oil and natural resources and tended to neglect the role of people in this regard. With the growth of the role of the media, it is crucial to initiate public awareness and education programmes. One of the prominent tasks of the mass media is to inform the public and improve society's political knowledge. As globalisation accelerates and we get closer to the idea of a world village, understanding the function and nature of the mass media is critical for preserving cultural identity and national values. It is noticeable that in spite of the Arab states' control over the mass media, these media are used to spread falsehood in society and when these lies are highlighted in the social media, the trust between the state and people deteriorates and must be addressed.

2. The government needs to supply a reliable source of information to the public and make it distinguishable from unreliable sources. Rumours are key features of the early days of a revolution. Corruption, the mistakes of those in authority, the recent measures of the government leading to nothing but extreme poverty are commonly spoken of in accusations in the Arab countries of the Middle East. Rumours are easily eliminated when the government enjoys public trust in its early days and keeps in touch with the public through official channels, as people are sure that before taking any measure their rulers will inform them. The point is that states in countries such as Iran and Saudi Arabia and other Arabic countries have developed such a negative image of the social media that they even deprive themselves of the advantages of this new possibility. It is notable that some experts and scholars believe that Obama won his recent election to the US presidency by his brilliant campaign in the social media. Another notable case is the Iranian

Foreign Minister's presence in the social networks in 2013 and 2014 talking directly to the people, reporting on nuclear negotiations with the West. His innovation was helpful in raising trust among the public. Before listening to rumours, people now go to social media to find out about recent developments.

3. The third step to be taken by the government is to let the people analyse the information they receive, which of course needs time. This step, however, does not need the state's permission, as people continuously analyse the information they receive about the government. The time needed for completion of this analysis does no favours for Arab governments, as every day a new aspect of the lies spread by those governments is revealed to the public. In democratic countries, however, this step is in favour of the government: the trust between the government and the people will grow as the honesty of the rulers is revealed for more citizens. It is noticeable that in spite of public dissatisfaction and negative evaluations of the government, the mass media in Iran and Saudi Arabia insist on broadcasting news that conveys the satisfaction of the people and the problems that people of other countries have to endure. This trend leads more unsatisfied groups to social media and may trigger revolution in the future.

4. The last step for the state is to use the evaluations made by the public regarding the state to improve its condition.

What is expected to result from taking these four steps is at least that no further revolution will take place and there will be a chance to resolve problems step by step. A review of the role of the dictators in Arab countries shows they use their power to control and suppress rather than as servants of the public to improve the livelihoods of their people. On the other hand, when the government has been weakened following the development of social media and other international changes, the system of suppression stands no chance and the increasing trend of denying the facts together with the growth of public dissatisfaction accelerate the pace of events. Given the experience among Islamic countries of being colonised by Western powers, the behaviour of Western leaders intensifies hatred towards the government. While dictatorships do not hesitate to employ the latest military technology from the West to suppress opposition, they impose limitations on the utilisation of other Western technologies, such as social media, under the pretext of protecting their culture and religion. Revolution is one of the consequences of this paradox. Needless to say, when civic institutes and social services bodies are weak there is no hope of society's regaining its true identity. By limiting the meaning and function of the state to suppression, what the state is left to deal with is a 'population' rather than a 'citizen'. This population is familiar with fear rather than loyalty. With fear the only gift of the government to the public, it is the underground and secret groups that have the capacity to fill the power gap when the government is weakened and its grip is loosened. This leads to anarchy and disorder and eventually revolution. Being headless was mentioned earlier as an advantage in the revolutions in Arab countries. However, in 2014 as this book is being written, the results of many of these revolutions is not clear, although one may conclude that the lack of a leader with political, informational and media literacy is why the revolutions have been misled. That is, where once it was an advantage, in the early days of the revolutions, being headless now is their weak point. Still, the utilisation of modern technologies is an unprecedented and exciting experience which has not as yet played out. The social media are still evolving and are continually taking new forms and aspects. These changes and the dynamism involved double the influence of the media and cover more and more groups of people. The effect of the social media is not limited to politics: areas such as the economy, commerce, recruitment, employment, support for customer rights, family, violence, accidents, civil laws, the fight against racial/sex discrimination, the struggle against crime and corruption, and support for transparency and responsiveness are included. People in Arab countries are observing the formation of a new world in which different laws take precedence, while new groups of people emerge that take control of the country for short periods of time. In short, one may say that any headless phenomenon is doomed to fail and Arab people have no reason, at least in the short run, to be happy with their revolution.

Media literacy and critical thinking

Having failed to control the accelerating developments in media and information technology, the target groups of the messages propagated by the media must expect deeper and more problematic changes in the future, as signals of such changes can already be seen.

Without media literacy it is not possible to make a proper selection among the messages received. In this regard, educational, civic and media institutions must improve media literacy to enable those addressed to have a deeper perception of what they hear, watch and read. People without media literacy are the main victims of the media industry, while others with such literacy are well aware of the media's tricks and are capable of reaching better judgements regarding their environment. The latter group is more effective in leading a revolution back on track. However, expecting a large portion of society to be equipped with media literacy is not realistic, as gaining such literacy needs a large set of skills which ordinary people do not possess. Still, the elites of society at least must develop media literacy. This is achievable when critical thinking in the people and the habit of accepting criticism in the government are developed. The term 'critical thinking' within the scope of media literacy has been noted by authors such as Worsnop (1989). People in the Arab countries under study complain that any criticism of their former government was countered, while they did not permit any criticism of their political party. This is one of the reasons why these revolutions take too long to accomplish. Those with media literacy tend not to accept whatever they see in the media and adopt a critical thinking stance – which is the key to media literacy – to analyse and evaluate what they hear and see. By 'critical thinking' we mean a process of checking and examining the authenticity and accuracy of information. To obtain this ability, one needs to avoid all cognitive mistakes and evaluate the authenticity and content of the information without prejudice or any influence from popular figures in society. In this way one can tell real news from fake. Critical thinking is one of the key elements of a liberal education that prepares people to take part in a dynamic society. One of the serious problems in Arab and Middle East countries that has guaranteed the survival of dictatorships in these countries is a lack of critical thinking among the people. Historical experience in different parts of the globe shows that through political choices not based on critical thinking the masses have always supported dictators. Critical thinking equips people to recognise populist and fake promises from the politicians and also avoid thoughtless adherence to others. The question here is whether social media have managed to improve critical thinking in Arab countries in such a short period. The answer is negative. People in Arab countries still lack critical thinking. They have used the social media as a place to express their criticism anonymously, as when a child breaks a window and runs away. This phenomenon can even pose a threat, as when anonymous people use the freedom to express radical opinions to join with and mislead others. Therefore, there is a lack of critical thinking in Arab countries and they have a long way to go to achieve media literacy. Here we need a measurement standard. To evaluate critical thinking among the Arab users of social media in the countries under study, a questionnaire with three factors and 14 indicators was designed; the results were as expected. The point obtained in all the countries under study was below the mean point, except in Tunisia, which is probably due to the education system in that country. Needless to say, more studies in this field are required. The results showed that Libya was at the bottom of the ranking of critical thinking by a significant margin. Again, the strict controls of Gaddafi's regime, which even influenced the education system of the country by dictating the content of textbooks, was to blame. Another feature of such an education system is a non-deductive curriculum based on memorisation, as is the case in Iran. It may be interesting for the readers of this book in Western countries that many university professors and students in Arab countries and Iran are proud of the extent of the content they have memorised, the books they have translated or philosophical books they have read. When acting and criticism are rejected, not even the development of social media can add to media literacy. New technologies are just new ways and opportunities for quasi-intellectual minds to show off, while the true opportunities of the technology are never discovered. This has been the case in Iran, according to the author's over twenty years of experience in the Iranian education system. With regard to the Arab countries, 61% of the respondents on average highlighted the non-deductive curriculum programming in schools and universities as the reason for the lack of critical thinking in these countries. This lack clearly explains the underdeveloped media literacy in these countries. To be recognised as having good characteristics is not enough to be a leader in a democratic country, which also needs insightful individuals capable of leading society. In fact, every individual with critical thinking is a leader. Living in society entails knowledge and the ability to express analytical criticism regarding social norms, culture, government systems, laws and social rules. Even the culture must avoid remaining stable and unchanged, as insightful citizens push through cultural changes. On the other hand, rulers in Arab countries tend to rely on their countries' several thousand years of rich culture to mislead the minds of the ctizens. The fact is that not even several thousand years of culture is enough to meet the needs of modern citizens. Realising the ideals of a democratic system depends on cultural development, social justice, the rule of law and the prosperity of mankind, which come about through bringing up citizens with the capability of critical thinking and analysing.

In addition to non-deductive bases of curriculum planning in the countries under study, there is another factor to the lack of media literacy – monopoly of the media. Generally, media literacy in developed countries is far more widespread and valued than in the third world or developing countries. A plurality of mass media is not the norm in developing countries and given that all messages are delivered by a few media from one source, media literacy is neglected. The monopoly of the regime over the mass media and the reluctance of rulers to improve media literacy are also common in developing countries and even the slightest movement in this regard is basically aimed at magnifying the voice of the ruler rather than developing media literacy. As a standard practice in developing countries, the movement toward the improvement of media literacy is actually aimed at influencing the messages delivered by foreign media and internal media are excluded; the internal media are presented as free of any error and it is only to resist the cultural invasion that people must be armed with media literacy.

The next point to mention is the role of media censorship in eliminating the need for media literacy. Arab governments and Iranian rulers, as a common practice, censor the news before it is broadcast, so the public no longer needs media literacy. However, with the emergence of the social media, the rulers have lost their grip on the media and now emphasise media literacy to fight back the invasion of enemies through social media. It is at this point that the actual process of media literacy is initiated, although its main purpose is to prop up the ruling system rather than improve public awareness. Doubtlessly censorship is also practised in Western countries, including the USA, but it is different from that in Arab countries, because students in the West are familiar with information literacy and critical thinking from an early age. Censorship of any kind in Arab countries triggers a specific type of analysis, based on the monopoly of the regime over the mass media, resulting in deeper mistrust of the system in society. On the other hand, censorship in the West never conveys the same meaning and in the worst cases people tend to blame the media, rather than the whole system. Loss of public trust in the state-run media prompts the public to refer to foreign media for news and information. Although, by doing this, they receive more reliable and authentic news and analysis, they risk a threat to their original culture and even to their religion and traditional roots. In this way one may conclude that self-censorship in Arab countries is one of the main factors in the rapid penetration of social media in the Arab countries' revolutions. Self-censorship is a sort of naturally preventive measure, which has mutated into a self-destructive measure with the advance of social media. Finding a neutral media with no dependency on any specific group and without censorship is almost impossible. As a result of the effects of political concerns on the mass media in Arab countries, group interests have overshadowed the interests of the wider society. At any rate, the social media are more or less semi-independent. Independent and critical media act as a safety valve and fulfil a critical role in the security and development of a country. Such media also support the ruling system against political, cultural and legitimacy threats, while preventing the accumulation of unmet demands among the public which may result in public riot. A committed media must work in favour of national and public interests by neglecting individual, group and party interests. Such media in Arab countries may convey to those who plunder the oil wealth how their actual interests are guaranteed by serving the public interest. The mass media in Arab countries are mainly state-run, while the outlook for media freedom is not promising. While Egypt is ranked by the World Press Freedom Index at 159 among 180 countries, none of the five Arab countries under study here have better conditions and more outbreaks of revolution seem unavoidable. Every member of these societies acts as a journalist who reports the events in a semi-free media.

References

Wallis, J. (2005). Cyberspace, information literacy and the information society. *Library Review*, *54*(4), 218–222.

Worsnop, C. M. (1989). *Media literacy through critical thinking*. Washington: NW Center for Excellence in Media Literacy. Available at: <http://depts.washington.edu/nwmedia/sections/nw_center/curriculum_docs/teach_combine.pdf> (retrieved September 2013).

Further reading

Witek, D., & Grettano, T. (2012). Information literacy on facebook: An analysis. *Reference Services Review*, *40*(2), 242–257.

Religious attitudes in the cyber world

5

Religion and media

In the previous chapter we said that religious activities constitute the main proportion of users' activities in social networks in the countries under study. This is also true among users of these networks in the USA. It appears at first glance that the emergence of mass media may address the status of religion, although there is nothing certain to prove this. Like any other social phenomenon, religion can employ social media for its own development, as can be seen on several religious websites. Another advantage of social media for religion is the easy expression of religious questions and attitudes and the facilitation of finding the answer. By its nature, religion is communicative as it comes from a source and is intended for human beings. Survival of the message depends on promotion in every direction, i.e. the message must be given to as many addressees as possible on the one hand, while on the other the addressees must contemplate the message. In this way, the message is protected from manipulation. Among the main characteristics of Middle Eastern countries are culture and religion, which also ensure the unity of the people. Naturally, the media in these countries have to be religious media. To imagine the role of media in this regard, compare a medium that has nothing to do with religion and another that promotes religious beliefs among its addressees. The fact that children watching the latter encounter religious thoughts explains the deep-seated role of the media in the formation of religious or anti-religious attitudes. Not surprisingly, people in the Middle East, the home of many great religions, expect religious messages from their media. For instance, in February 2014 the Iranian Supreme Leader's website was ranked as the 235th most visited website in the country, while by 12 April 2014 this ranking was 152nd. The same tendency to religion and continuing expansion of Islam through the mass media has fuelled fears of Islam among Western media. Undoubtedly other religions such as Christianity are expanding and there are even cases of conversion to Christianity among Muslims in Iran. However, the media competition between Islam and Christianity is not a fair fight. For instance, the persistent depiction in the West of Muslims as terrorists feeds the fear in the West and the attempts to stop the expansion of Islam in the West and the Middle East, and justifies the ventures of the West in the region. To gain an equal position in the competition, Islam must use the media to fight back the media invasion from the West. Thus religion uses the media for expansion, but when the media explicitly serves the religion revolution ensues. In fact, religion not only uses the media to promote its values, it also influences its function and behaviour. The extent of the influence depends on the acceptance of religion and the fields covered by religion. In this

Online Arab Spring.

regard, a religion which claims to have a programme for every aspect of human life considers itself entitled (and responsible) to prescribe recommendations and requirements. In addition, censorship also becomes one of its main features. Note that religion must be isolated from other indices mentioned in previous chapters. Religion is actually a background against which other indices function, so that people coordinate their activities in the social media based on their religion. Nevertheless, social media add an index to religion. The testability and performance of religion in social media is evident and easy to ensure. In spite of the mass media, interactive media provide an opportunity to promote religion and prove religious beliefs. However, among Muslims, religious people tend to be reluctant to use new technologies. There are two main explanations for this. First, supporters of Islam, for instance in Iran, are also the supporters of the (religious) government and to protect itself the government tries to keep the public from using modern technologies and keep their political awareness to a minimum. Secondly, Islam advises man to avoid sin and relationships beyond the framework of the religion. The Internet is a 'bad technology', as it facilitates easy relationships between people. Thus, technology is classified by religious states as good and bad. In this way, opponents of Islam have enough time to employ new technologies to mislead Islamic societies, while Muslims are busy discussing their advantages and disadvantages. This gap is not filled even when religious Muslims accept social media and learn how to use technology by trial and error in favour of their religion.

Islam, media and fighting oppression

Many believe that the tyranny of the rulers was one of the main reasons for the recent revolutions in Arab countries. Given that the majority of the population of the Arab countries are Muslim and that Islam always emphasises fighting oppression, in many cases these revolutions have been named 'Islamic Awakening' and specific movements have tried to exaggerate their ties with the public movements. Although using this term to describe the revolutions does not seem too inappropriate, by doing so many other aspects of the revolutions are neglected. On the other hand, the term 'Arab Spring' can also convey the idea of 'Islamic Awakening', without neglecting other factors. If we take 'Islamic Awakening' as appropriate to describe the recent revolutions and these revolutions follow the path of the Islamic Revolution in Iran, the question is, why did it take 35 years for the Arab nations to adopt this model of revolution? It must be admitted that regardless of the region, any nation that suffers oppression to such an extent would challenge their government through social media if they could. That is, the same phenomenon could be expected in other parts of the world if the building blocks were available. What drove the Arab revolutions was political awareness and the opportunity to oppose the government in social media anonymously. What we have here is leadership of a revolution by social media against a religious background (regardless of the nature of the religion). If the Arab revolutions follow the path of the Islamic Revolution in

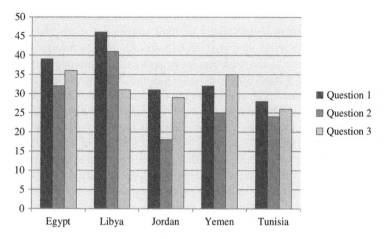

Figure 5.1 Percentage of positive answers to the three questions.

Iran, where is the religious leader – someone like Imam Khomeni in Iran – to keep these revolutions on track? If the movements in the Arab countries were following a specific path, they would be on another one now. The fact is, these revolutions do not follow any model and stray away from their goals through trial and error. They may become a comprehensive model for future revolutions after relative successes. Suppose that these movements in Arab countries have Islamic roots, just as many other revolutions in other parts of the world are rooted in poverty and low welfare standards. The question is, why would the Arab nations adopt an Islamic revolution while they can see that poverty and big differences between in social classes in other Islamic societies are growing? Is it reasonable to assume that the Arab nations would have followed a path which they knew was doomed to fail? In the following sections, we bring in evidence to show that an Islamic state was not the intention of the movements in Arab nations (see Figure 5.1). Three questions were put to the respondents:

1. Do you participate in the movement to establish an Islamic system?
2. Do you think that only an Islamic state can bring dignity back to your country?
3. Do you think that an Islamic state can realise the goals for which you joined the revolution?

About 3,000 respondents from different countries answered these questions and the results clarified some aspects; however, we do not claim that the respondent group is perfectly representative of the study population. Only positive answers are plotted and clearly Libya has the highest rate of positive response to the first two questions. It is notable that there were more negative answers to these questions than positive answers in all countries. It is undeniable that Islamist tendencies were never absent in the Islamic countries of the Middle East. Let us compare the movement in the Arab countries and the unrest of 2009 in Iran. Iran is an Islamic country and apparently a successful case of revolution – although we did mention earlier that it has diverged from its preliminary objectives to some extent. Faced with growing poverty and a reduction in public welfare, the Iranian people rioted in 2009, claiming that the election results were fraudulent and that the current government was only making poverty worse. One may say that the unrest in Iran, which was led by social media, brought with it the idea of revolution from other Arab countries. Although the 2009 unrest in Iran was suppressed by the government, the fact that people opposed the state and not Islamic rule was undeniable. This can be seen in the recent presidency election of 2013 in Iran, where many voted for change in the state. Thus it is the state, rather than the ruling system, that deals with the public. Many of those who took part in riots against the system in 2009 decided to vote in 2013, even though they knew that nothing in the system was going to change. In this case, the people perceived that they could enjoy more welfare and achieve a reduction in poverty by changing the state, regardless of the ruling system. Such behaviour can be seen in developed countries as social reforms come about by replacing the ruling party while the whole system remains intact. Therefore, even if an Islamic party does take power in an Arab country, this does not mean that an Islamic movement will emerge. It means rather that people believe that Islam can bring stability to the country. By the same token, voting for a non-Islamic party does not mean that the public is drawn to Western ideology or resents Islam. The fact that fewer than 50% of the respondents were positive about Islamic government probably means that they think their current government is not truly Islamic. Many probably believe that the idea of an Islamic government may not go further than superficial changes to the ruling system, while corruption is never eradicated. They know that Islam is only a cover for the corrupt system. If that is not so, why does no one say that the unrest of 2009 in Iran was a sort of Islamic awakening? It is true that the unrest was triggered by elections, but it was actually a reaction to widespread corruption in an Islamic country where Islam is only another means of suppression and tyranny. The Islam that Iranian people wanted was supposed to bring prosperity in this world and the next. At any rate, given that the majority of the Arab people are Muslims and supporting unity is one of the features of Islam, no one can deny the key role of Islam in the recent revolutions in Arab countries. The Islamic and non-Islamic movements of the Arab Spring are now trying to find a new beginning.

There is an undeniable paradox in the claim of Islamic awakening. The proponents of this idea go further, claiming that the 'Islamic Awakening' movement is not limited to the Islamic countries of the Middle East and Africa but will gradually extend to Europe and America. A widespread opposition movement in the West known as the 'Occupy Movement' – the best known instance being 'Occupy Wall Street' – brought thousands of European and American citizens to the street to protest against economic conditions, the gaps between social classes and injustice and to call for change. Is this an Islamic awakening? When it comes to Islamophobia, the rulers of Islamic countries, including Iran, claim that Western media promote Islamophobia and depict people from the Middle East and Muslims as terrorists. But when it comes to riots in the West, Westerners who are supposed to be anti-Islamist follow the Islamic Awakening and trigger the 'Occupy Wall Street' movement. What is this if not a paradox? Doubtless Islam is capable of finding supporters in the West, but to claim that 'Occupy Wall Street' or the unrest in Ukraine are Islamic movements we need first to find the essential building blocks and background. These building blocks include a strong Islamic media in the West, fighting against Islamophobia, introducing true Islam to the West, and even Islamic rulers' acknowledgement of their failure to bring Islam into practice. People in the West need to see in practice that establishment of real Islam in Islamic countries has led to general cultural, political and economic development. Clearly no Islamic ruler would ever admit this, as it marks the end of their glorious sovereignty. To shed more light on the issue, let us name some of the features of an Islamic ruling system and see if the Iranian system of rule, which claims that Arab revolutions were inspired by the Iranian revolution, is truly an Islamic system or not. The prominent characteristic of an Islamic system is the implementation of social justice. Among the indicators of social justice, only education in Iran is at an acceptable level, while other indicators, such as the gap between the poor and the wealthy and the human development index, are disappointing. In the Human Development Index of 2013, Iran is ranked 76th, while no Islamic country is among the top 20.[1] Why shouldn't we call for a 'Christianity Awakening'? If the purpose of rebellion in the Arab countries is to achieve welfare and social justice, why should they follow the path of a country that 35 years after its revolution is still nowhere close to social justice? Why not follow Norway, for instance, a country at the top of the social justice list, free of poverty, politically stable and with no worries about corruption among the authorities? The only basis for calling the Arab national movement an 'Islamic Awakening' is that the majority of the population are Muslim. However, the point is that they are not fighting for an *Islamic* tomorrow but rather for a *better* tomorrow. Being better does not necessarily mean being Islamic, although adopting an indigenous solution that fits the national culture and religion is understandable. Another point to mention is that people with the same inputs have different outputs in Iran, a cause that intensifies social gaps. Still, we must not neglect the effect of the West's sanctions against Iran, which have created a heaven for a few to exploit. Here, sanctions, along with poor legal structures and supervision, have increased the social gap. In addition, people in Iran are not treated equally by the law. The second prominent feature of an Islamic society – equality before law – is absent in Iran, as is evidenced by the large-scale financial corruption of recent years.

The corruption of the authorities in Arab countries has always been a problem and recent disclosures of corruption by the social media served to intensify the revolutions. Arab countries have no reason to follow the Islamic revolution in Iran when Iran is not even close to achieving the first goals of those revolutions.

Religion and social media: a mutual relationship

It appears that it is religion that employs the media to promote itself, but the fact is the media also use religion as a way of developing and attracting more users. Search the word 'religion' on the Internet to see how many websites and social media have gained their reputation and popularity on the back of this single word. Thousands of users only sign up for religious purposes so these websites enjoy higher advertisement rates. Religion is not only used by social media: Arab and Middle Eastern countries have long experience of employing religion for other purposes. In the past, the *minbar* (where a clergyman sits in the mosque and addresses the people) was a medium for promoting Islam and whoever sat there had to be a knowledgeable Islamic scientist. However, the knowledge and beliefs of those who post or promote ideas in the social media are not clear. Thus the religious content in social media can be helpful or misleading, as many newly emerged religions are using the advantages of social media and are better than traditional religions at using modern technologies. At any rate, using the media is the best way to the universalisation of religions. It is clear from Islamic training that it is a universal religion and has never stopped trying to be a universal religion throughout its history. Other divine religions also have the same claim: Christianity, for instance, claims to be the only way to the divine and does not limit itself to any specific group of people or region. History books clearly show the different promotional approaches taken by religions at different times and in different places. In addition, belief in the 'End Time Saviour' is common among people of different religions. What might challenge the revolutions in Arab countries in the trend toward globalisation is the preservation of cultural identity. These revolutions, on the one hand, are supposed to protect national traditions and establish legal, educational, social, economic and political systems, while on the other hand they have to face the rapid changes of modernisation and the adoption of technological tools and institutions. That is, they must always be ready to face invasion by other cultures. The technology-facilitated revolutions in the Arab countries originated in the West and in the USA in particular, but the concept of technology is not a familiar one in the East. Still, the youth in Arab counties have widely accepted the new technologies and the West can use the technology to raise a generation that serves the West's interests. Therefore, despite a considerable decrease in the presence of Western powers in the Middle East, they have managed to strengthen their cultural effect. This cultural influence leads Islam in Arab countries towards American-style Islam, which is partly based on divine training and partly based on Western training and thus is not quite like true Islam and not quite like Western ideology. In other words, neither true Islam nor the simple rule of technology can be found in Middle Eastern countries and now and again these two trends have become controversial. This is another factor that waters down the role of specific countries in the region, e.g. Iran and the Arab countries, as these countries do not enjoy the cultural influence of the West, nor they do they have the requisite tools.

Religious democracy from a new viewpoint

The question is then whether religion can be the ground for revolution in the modern world? There is no definite answer to this, but even if religion is not the main ground for revolution in the Arab countries, it at least prepares the ground. In fact the roles of religion and the social media in preparing the ground for revolution cannot be disentangled. As argued before, it is not possible to convince the majority of people in Arab countries to establish a religious and Islamic state. Thus the term 'religious democracy' – participation of the people in government, their affairs and managing the society based on religion – as widely used by Iranian rulers, cannot be properly applied to Arab countries. The fact is that establishing a religious state is not the goal of the Arab movements, but rather establishing a government that realises their goals against a religious background. This ensures that religion cannot be utilised as a tool to gain power and cover up corruption and at the same time the distinction between religion and government is preserved and observed. People in Iran live under the rule of a system which claims Islam is its first priority. When the Iranian people hear about corruption in government authorities and financial problems they begin simultaneously to accuse their government and Islam, as the two are entwined. Note that we do not support secularism here. According to the novel approach of religious democracy, when the Muslim nation is allowed to supervise and question the government, the religious values of Islam will gradually enter its policies. However, if the Islamic government assumes that it is authorised by God and finds itself responsible to society even for the smallest of things, corruption of the system is inevitable. In this case, any attempt by the people to reform the system will be construed as divergence from religion, even if the public movement is based on religious codes. Under the rule of God, any movement for freedom means disagreement with God, Islam and the order of the Quran, and must be suppressed. Therefore no improvement regarding freedom of speech can be expected. In this way, religious democracy – based on the novel approach – is democracy in religious terms that can rebuild the true power of Islam and change the negative attitudes of the West to Islam. This new concept is realised when the two factors of a coup against a tyrannical ruler and the quest to improve the role of the people in power and public reluctance to establish religious government are mixed. Proponents of religious democracy and straight democracy each accuse the other system of being a new way to dictatorship. One can say this, at least, that supremacy of one over another person is rooted in achievements, while under religious democracy, the road to dictatorship is paved with the claim to be religious and the promise of heaven, so that supremacy of one over another is justified, even when nothing has been achieved.

Religious meritocracy

Clear cases of religious dictatorship are Iran, Saudi Arabia and Bahrain as they deny one of the primary religious principles – meritocracy. That is, between 'commitment' and 'knowledge', which are two key features of meritocracy, the former is overemphasised. Countries that believe solidly in commitment argue that emphasis on expertise and knowledge is the starting point in the decline of a society.

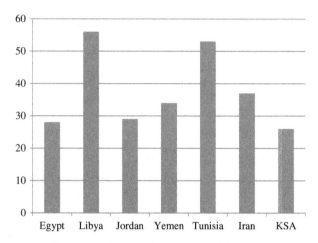

Figure 5.2 Percentage of positive answers to the question about meritocracy.

Therefore they have sharp eyes for terms such as 'development' and whatever supports this tendency is bad. Now consider another key feature of the respondents' attitude which was explored by the question 'to what extent do you think that the ruling system of your country observe meritocracy?' It is notable that Iran in this regard is a symbol of religious meritocracy while Saudi Arabia is expecting revolution.

Figure 5.2 represents many facts. Saudi Arabia is at the bottom regarding meritocracy, which makes the rulers of the country worry about the stability of their government as they lack public support. Something less than 40% of the respondents believed in meritocracy in Iran, which again hints at the unstable position of the ruling system in that country. Although the new government and election of Dr Rouhani increased public hope for change, it is worth repeating the poll in Iran after the recent presidential election.

One point which is usually neglected is that commitment is a qualitative index and even in Iran people only try to appear to be committed in the hope of promotion to higher positions. However, in many cases, it is found that people who are apparently committed to religious beliefs are morally corrupt. Expressing commitment to religious codes simply to gain a higher position evolves into corruption in the system as people of higher rank tend not to use knowledgeable people in their organisation, as such people highlight the incompetency of their supervisors. This is a sort of state religion which is nowhere close to religious government, which would extend justice in the society.

Islamic political parties

Another question to ask is why political parties such as the Muslim Brotherhood in Egypt and the Ennahda Movement in Tunisia kept their power for a while after the revolution in their country? Clearly, the main cause of this is the long history of Islam in these countries and that these parties emphasise the expansion of justice and the fight against corruption. Now these parties have found their place in social media through many official and unofficial pages. Still, the number of 'Likes' and 'Followers' of these parties shows that they do not possess a unique position in social media. On the other hand, the Muslim Brotherhood is a relative supporter of freedom of speech so that it finds alignment between Islam and supporting freedom. These tendencies have resulted in the isolation of this party among the other Islamic parties in the long run. In spite of the unsuccessful experiences of the traditional parties in social media, emerging parties have a distinctive appearance in social media so that some of the recently established parties have emerged as the main rivals of the Muslim Brotherhood and attracted many to their pages by adopting popular slogans. The failure of the old Muslim parties hints at the lack of political experience that makes them the losers within a few months of the revolution. Let us focus on the subject of this book. What features do the Islamic parties need to have to keep their supporters in social media? We are not talking about the general preferred features that any political party needs to have. We are only talking about Muslim political parties in Arab countries and the results are not generally applicable for every political party. In contrast to other parts of the study, which were based on quantitative methods, here qualitative methods, open-ended questionnaires and coded indices were used and, afterward, the final indices were obtained through quantitative methods. Here we only discuss the indices. The most important question in this section is: 'What indices can be effective in the success of an Islamist party in the Arab countries of the Middle East and North Africa in social media? The following indices answer how Islamic parties can defeat their rivals in the social media. The indices are not listed in order of priority and while some are applicable to social media, others are applicable to the real world.

Respecting the tribal structure of Arab countries in social media

Surprisingly the results showed that tribal structures must be respected by the Islamic parties in social media. Arab countries retain strong tribal ties in spite of the expansion of new technologies in these countries. Therefore, by supporting people's tribal and cultural ties, political parties can improve their popularity in social media, even if Islam is not a key concern of those parties. Cultural globalisation has expanded, with amazing consequences, over the countries of the region following the development of media technologies such as satellite channels and the Internet. Among the key consequences of this trend are the weakening of tribal ties and improvement of the concept of citizenship. However, these changes cannot erase the thousands years of history of these tribes. These countries have decided to achieve a mutual agreement between technology and tradition. Fast economic growth powered by crude oil and the export of raw materials has resulted in considerable social changes such as population growth, the emergence of a new social life, the growth of an educated population and the purchase of technology (rather than transferring technology). This externally induced modernism has no cultural congruity. It is imported mainly from the West and many countries of the region are influenced by the changes, so that the negative effects of these changes have always been a concern for the people of the region and scientists. Probably one of the reasons for emphasising tribal ties in social media is this concern. Following a fast transition period and the introduction of modern technologies to Arab countries, many of the respondents highlighted the fact that, in the same way as other cultures influence Arab culture, through the expansion of these technologies Arab culture soon will be able to influence and even defeat that of the West.

Supporting cultural reconstruction

Many respondents believed that the tendency of Islamic political parties to align with Western culture was one of the reasons for their failure in policy. They noted that Islamic political parties are now competing in the social media, which is another new Western way to sell their traditional and cultural beliefs. The strategy has proved to be useless, as the method they have chosen for the purpose has overshadowed their aim. Debates on the Internet between political parties and their supporters are lengthier and there is less exchange of ideas between users. One reason for this may be the fact that communication is not completely written, nor completely oral, but rather a mixture of the two. People participating in computer-based communication tend to express different ideas from those they usually believe. The increase in the users' capabilities to accept and tolerate other cultures and people via the Internet extends the culture of tolerance over the social system and creates a new culture in the long run, without any history. By supporting the primary culture of the users, Islamic political parties can improve their role in social networks.

Popular parties

The social media have provided an unprecedented opportunity for public participation in political parties. However, the respondents expressed the view that parties are formed by a few founders, who then try to gain the support of the public. Then it is their goals, and not the public interest, that are followed by the party. We did not find a party popular across the board among the countries under study and people were mainly worried about their irrational participation in the party. Indeed, since the parties are not formed based on national interests, they can never enjoy wide public support. The establishment of parties in Arab countries is top-down, so that they do not arise out of society but rather are state-built parties, which only try to support the government. Another important point is that the security of people after accepting membership of a political party is not guaranteed. The fact that studies, jobs and social activities might be jeopardised prevents many from entering a political party. This is mostly the case when the party is not an independent popular party. Therefore, independent and popular Islamic parties can help the development of parties in Arab countries.

Emphasis on economy

The history of Arab countries and Iran indicates that economic growth stops or barely grows when an Islamist party takes over power in the country. A clear case of this is the fundamentalists in Iran. Being one-dimensional is the main challenge ahead for the development of Islamic parties. This makes them defenceless before the parties that emphasise economic concerns, which are in turn brutally attacked when they fail to realise their economic promises owing to lack of experience. People in Arab countries believe that reacting emotionally to the economic slogans of parties is in the past. For instance, accurate analyses of the factors contributing to economic underdevelopment are of more interest than simply promises of economic development. Results from the responses to one of the questions by participants from the five countries indicated that 37% of the respondents have stopped supporting their parties within the last two years. One reason for this disloyalty is that the parties are incapable of achieving their primary goals, and their economic goals in particular.

Using public power in the media

Regardless of the number of supporters of a social media page, it is effective only when the party is able to use the page to send its messages to the supporters. In one of the latest instances of this, Narendra Modi, a prime ministerial candidate in India with three million followers on Twitter, employed hundreds of volunteers to distribute his message over the social media.[2] He is an opponent of Islamists in India. Still, his successful experience can be a motivation for Islamic parties to use their supporters to promote their ideas as Islam as a religion has been very successful in using promoters. There is a proverb about the importance of social media: 'The key to success in social networks is to win the support of many.' However, we strongly reject this with regard to political and social media and parties. It only takes a few seconds to become a 'Follower' or 'Like' a page and many of these messages of support are not based on a deep belief in the ideology of the party. The real supporters are those who bother to spread the message of the party. To shed more light on the issue, think about business matters in social media. The fact is that political parties need to adopt a strategy to use the energy of the users as do businesses.

Despite several advantages of social media and access to a wide range of customers who use the media, many companies are reluctant to enter the field, as they see no need to do so and assume it would be negligence of their values (Grainger, 2010). The same traditional thinking can be traced among political parties, so that they prefer paper advertisements and posters to digital pages. On the other hand, there are two trends of changes that are leading to fundamental changes in economic and social activities. The first is the exponential expansion of electronic networks and the second is the creation of value by digital technologies for individuals and organisations (Vuori, 2012; Agarwal, Gupta, & Kraut, 2008). However, current businesses are still looking for strategies to deal with the social media. They also try to control the communication environment within a control network to ensure that their brand and message are available and seen everywhere. However, people usually have more of a sense of ownership over their pages in the virtual society and develop negative attitudes toward any firm that they think has breached their privacy (Palmer and Koenig-Lewis, 2009; Hitwise, 2008). It is critical for the development of political parties for them to use the power of individuals to protect their privacy. In the not too distant past organisations tended to use direct strategies to communicate with their customers and users, a method which has no support nowadays. It is notable that people do not enter social media to become members of political parties, but rather to find their friends and express their ideas more freely. Therefore digital membership of a political party is not the first priority. One of the strategy researchers (Piskorski, 2011) said that digital strategy means spreading commercial messages and facilitating marketing and sales. In fact, it is a way to let customers have direct contact with the company. However, social strategy is aimed at exposing potential clients to the messages of the company indirectly and through their interaction with other clients rather than the company. In fact, a digital strategy is converted to a social strategy when it enters a social environment and tries to connect people to each other. The key to the success of political parties in an electronic environment is using individuals to promote their messages, rather than sending messages directly to the users.

Selecting the correct form of media

Although it is generally said that social media are a way to cut the cost of reaching the users, failure to select the correct form of media is a waste of these cost reductions. Therefore it is important to select the media based on the nature of the message. Factors in selecting the proper type of media are discussed in Chapter 6. As a general result, respondents expressed that their preferred forms of media are online news sites, video and audio, regardless of the social media (e.g. Facebook, Twitter, YouTube and so on). It is noticeable that the respondents wanted to get their ideas across via publishing and blogging more than by word of mouth.

Using social media as a strategic analysis tool

Strategic analysis is the first tool of strategic management, on which are based other steps in strategic management, e.g. selection, execution and strategic assessment. A set of logical activities is notable in strategic analysis, including spotting opportunities and risks in the available solutions. Strategic analysis demands a comprehensive analysis of the internal and external environment of the organisation. Such analysis can be done by one or several analysers (strategic team) and the results obtained can be used as a reliable base for setting and selecting strategies in the future. However, determining the four fields of strengths, weaknesses, opportunities and threats (SWOT) for political parties is not as straightforward as for businesses. For instance, assume 1,000 individuals have volunteered to promote the ideas of a party. One way is to classify these volunteers in the 'strengths' field; however, they can be also a 'weakness', 'opportunity' or 'threat' if they only 'follow' or 'like' the page of the party. In addition, volunteers chosen from Muslims and followers of other religions can be an advantage or disadvantage. Another key point in doing the analysis is to carefully select the stakeholders of the party. That is, an Islamist party does not necessarily need to have Muslim stakeholders, and dealing with the diverging interests of the stakeholders needs revision of the slogan and messages chosen by the Islamist party.

Financial support in social media

A notable point regarding the responses is that on the one hand the individuals more committed to the party are more likely to support the party financially, and on the other hand, having extended financial support, the members feel more commitment to the party, as they now supply both financial resources and loyalty. The respondents mentioned two key factors, the development of commitment to an Islamist party in the social media and the consequent increase of financial support for the party.

Financial transparency

When the main goal of the party is to improve justice and the realisation of its slogans there is no reason for a lack of financial transparency. Otherwise, the main financial supporters of the party become the key stakeholders of the party when they take power and the rest of the stakeholders are neglected. Transparency is one of the most important attractions of the party and also one of the main elements within the leadership of the parties. The extent of transparency is a function of the tendency and capability of the management of the party to remove any distinction from other parties in this regard. In fact, the parties that fail to meet transparency standards are too risky for their leaders. Such parties may lose public trust and develop a bad reputation in this regard. For Islamic parties that claim Islam rejects financial corruption this is not just a tool to win public trust but rather a duty that proves their legitimacy.

Proving the necessity of the party

In total, 57% of respondents argued that parties cannot realise their slogan promising democracy and justice. What is the point of being committed to a party when it cannot prove its practicality and advantage? The question is, what advantage can be realised for the stakeholders of a party via social media? Unfortunately, social media have only been used as a communication tool between the parties and their stakeholders. We need to determine the advantages of social media and which aspects of a party's activities can enjoy them. After strategic analyses, the first step to be taken by a party is to prepare a political programme by means of which a logical link between mid-term and long-term goals is ensured. The key indices of such a programme can be negotiated and revised by the party and the stakeholders and social media can facilitate this process. The actual role of social media in this regard is to reform. In addition, assume that before the presidential election in Egypt and the election of Mohammad Morsi people could have chosen one candidate among several through social media. Do you think that the first government in Egypt after the revolution would have had the same fate? It is notable that elements of the unrest during Morsi's administration were due to the wrong policies and decisions. As the next step, the parties must employ social media as an educational tool. Loyal stakeholders must learn about the principles of the party and the effect of advertisements by other parties must be minimised by daily education regarding changes in the party. One of the main causes of the failure of Islamist parties is their lack of political experience, which is probably due to poor education. Politicians reach higher levels of decision-making in the parties without receiving the necessary education. Education measures taken by parties must act as a screening stage in the party, just as school students have to pass final exams before going on to higher levels. Education to improve media literacy was discussed in previous sections; however, the nature of education for party members is unique, and is quite different from public education. Education outside the party must be aligned with the interests of different parts of the society and based on the education level of target groups. The capacity of social media to detect the educational level of different groups can be helpful. On the other hand, market segmentation to send different messages via social media marks a difference from how things were in the past. In Iran, for instance, market segmentation is based on reformist and fundamentalist wings; before sending their messages these two wings must prepare different messages for the different target groups. The main indices for classifying the political market in social media will be discussed in Chapter 6. Geographic and demographic variables are not so effective for political segmentation in the social media, while the level of behavioural, psychological and media education among followers and leaders can be more effective to this end. As far as our surveys showed, even religion cannot be a reliable index for political segmentation in social media, as people's behaviour in a virtual environment is barely related to religion. Individuals in the real world tend to follow religious codes to express their dependency on religious parties, while in virtual space people can appear with a fake identity and be what they really want to be. All these factors indicate that the mere deployment of liberal and democratic slogans does not justify the existence of political parties in social media and different social groups must be provided with different messages.

Political crisis management

Social media are considered by the former tyrannical governments of Arab countries to represent a crisis. But nowadays, in addition to presenting a crisis for the political parties, social media can be a tool for crisis management. A crisis can be understood to be the outcome of the spread of unfavourable news or the loss of control over events, rather than intentional and planned measures and decisions. It has been mentioned in previous chapters that Arab countries, following the outbreak of crises, experienced a sudden increase in the number of social media users for a short period of time. The same trend was followed in Iran and Saudi Arabia. However, unrest was controlled in the latter and faced brutal suppression in Iran. Clearly, public movements and behaviour can be early-warning indicators, but the question is, what must the reaction be? In most cases of political unrest, people have the wrong image of the capabilities of the government, owing to inappropriate promotion by competitors. At this level, informing the public in real time on social media can be a means to control political movements and political parties can have the upper hand, whether to support or attack the state, using their followers. The whole power of the social media emerges at this level and the parties which have trained, well-committed followers can enjoy the maximum capabilities of the social media acting as a mediator. However, this only happens when party ties are not too strong, as otherwise the power of the political party may overcome the social media, which are mainly used as a tool in the hands of the party.

Integration of the political parties' supply chain

It is the use of the social media as a way to access all sections of a party, down to its fundamentals, that is regarded as a winning formula. Owing to environmental pressures, the party may stray from its original constitution over time; however, if the party is always supervised by the public, this is less likely to happen. An important point that is always forgotten by parties is that, like commercial businesses, they have a supply chain which assures their survival, a chain that begins with the financial and intellectual sponsors and pressure groups, and encompasses the people and adherents. However, while sponsors have always been a priority for parties, today's financial sponsors are not able to have a significant role in parties' survival. Thus the intellectual sponsors' role has been greatly enhanced and 'crowdsourcing' now provides a suitable means for value creation, for both a party and the public. In these two concepts, all of the beneficiaries of the party would play an active role in its promotion and the parties, while observing users' recommendations in the social media, would act in such a way that shared value is created and loyalty to the party considerably increased in the long term. Thus, nowadays, setting a single goal for the party cannot result in its survival, so this goal must be designed in way that is accepted by more beneficiaries. For instance, when a Muslim party proceeds to create value through crowdsourcing, not only will Muslims be compatible with it, but also other religions, because the shared values are beyond religion. Thus, accepting the principle that there are shared values between believers and the divine religions, based on what can be discussed, is one of the most important conditions on which to reach agreement and get past the circumstances of dissension, confrontation and conflict. Various forms of dialogue have existed between religions throughout history, with which some have struggled and from which others have withdrawn. Now, with widespread and complex relationships and the global community, it is not possible to seclude oneself and withdraw from others. Thus the social media are an instrument to reinforce a political party through the strengthening of religions and not their separation. As mentioned earlier, public movements in different countries have campaigned for justice. Such movements have included Muslims and non-Muslims, whether or not there is a paradox whereby the values of Christianity can promote those of Islam.

The advantages of creating shared values among political parties through crowd-sourcing are as follows:

- Making sense of the usefulness of the lowest level of users and advocates of the parties.
- Building loyalty to the parties in the case of exchange (and implementation) of ideas with the users (and running the risk that if their ideas are not implemented in the long term, the users would come to the conclusion that the only role that they play is a theoretical one, that their ideas will never see the light of day and that such a party only has the appearance of being friendly).
- Building critical thinking among users and improving their level of media literacy.
- Preventing critical and other possible challenges. In fact, when people engage in crowdsourcing they manifest a dark side that can in the future create a crisis that the parties have to remedy in sufficient time.
- Although it is possible that all of the individuals who participate in crowdsourcing are not really adherents of that party, the degree of their participation in this trend is regarded as a cold war between the parties, and the party which can attract more political involvement in the crowdsourcing would have more bargaining power.
- This approach can make consensus possible among people who may not really even be involved in the election. Many people on social media are not of legal age for involvement in an official election and others, for whatever reason, are not ready to participate. However, crowdsourcing, which is a type of informal process to create political involvement, makes all members of society into political activists, who of course have a lot of strengths and weaknesses.

Some of the points made above are recommendations for Islamic parties, while others are useful for all political parties. In conclusion, it is possible to observe the use of social media by political parties. However, this needs the provision of infrastructure such as support for the tribal system among the people, improvement in commitment and loyalty to parties and accurate strategic analysis. Like businesses, parties have to answer to stakeholders and failure to meet the interests of these stakeholders brings in the process of brand development. By using social media as a tool for brand development, traditional Islamist parties can emerge at an international level.

Notes

1. http://hdr.undp.org/sites/default/files/reports/14/hdr2013_en_complete.pdf
2. http://www.dw.de/indias-political-parties-embrace-social-media/a-17410388

References

Agarwal, R., Gupta, A. K., & Kraut, R. (2008). Editorial overview – the interplay between digital and social networks. *Information Systems Research, 19*(3), 243–252.
Grainger, J. (2010). Social media and the fortune 500: How the fortune 500 uses, perceives and measures social media as a marketing tool. MA thesis, University of North Carolina at Chapel Hill, School of Journalism and Mass Communication.

Hitwise. (2008). *The impact of social networking in the UK.* Available at: <http://www. bergenmediaby.no/admin/ressurser/QCetFnO$_11_Social_Networking_Report_2008.pdf> Accessed 2.04.09.

Palmer, A., & Koenig-Lewis, N. (2009). An experiential, social network-based approach to direct marketing. *Direct Marketing: An International Journal, 3*(3), 162–176.

Piskorski, M. (2011). Social strategies that work. *Harvard Business Review*, November.

Vuori, M. (2012). Exploring uses of social media in a global corporation. *Journal of Systems and Information Technology, 14*(2), 155–170.

Country-social media intelligence: towards a new index

6

Social media intelligence

All concepts that are discussed in this chapter relate to the country and government and not to political parties; however, parties can use the concepts where appropriate. Note that, owing to the specialised nature of the concepts discussed in this chapter, the questionnaire was not distributed among the public to confirm the indices and trends. Instead, the comments of 16 experts in the fields of marketing, sociology, political marketing and social media have been incorporated. The concept of social media intelligence is defined at the governmental level as follows: the ability to predict the behaviour of beneficiaries and lead them to the political goals of the government. However, the words 'social intelligence', which are at the root of this definition, have long been defined by Thorndike (1920) and Wawra (2009) as follows: 'the ability to understand and manage men and women, boys and girls – to act wisely in human relationships'. However, this definition is at the individual level and what is needed is far beyond that. In fact, we are trying to extend this definition in order to understand the political behaviour of individuals in a social media environment, and accordingly try to predict and change their behaviour, or, in line with the available information, make the best decision. In this case, there is a problem because there is the intermediary of social media technology between the beneficiaries and our technology. This behaviour is not something that we would normally see, but it can be feigned and may be far from the individual's usual behaviour in a physical environment. Therefore we must find those indices that can shape the behaviour of individuals in a virtual environment. However, there are some advantages for the behaviour of individuals in a technological environment. People's behaviour can be traced in a social media environment and particularly in social networks. For instance, any previous data that has been published by a person on social media can be considered a predictor of their behaviour. According to our study, people's behaviour in the Internet environment is usually more stable than in the physical environment because our behaviour in a physical environment is also a function of our friend's or partner's behaviour. For instance, it is possible to exhibit a behaviour to please our partner in a certain set of circumstances that is not really in conformity with who we are, but there is no such limitation in the Internet environment. Therefore, contrary to what is expected, that a behaviour has further complications in a covert environment, we contend that such a behaviour assumes a greater simplicity that reflects the actual nature of individuals more than ever. Despite this simplicity, people try to show themselves at their best: only 26 per cent

Online Arab Spring.

of 1,507 people in Iran and the other five Arab countries believed that they would try to portray themselves differently from their real self. This percentage is highly significant and it can at least be hoped that the majority of individual behaviours exhibited in social and imaginary media are honest and can be relied on. When these factors are considered at the national level, country-social media intelligence (CSMI) will help governments predict future movements among the people and protesters so that they can take appropriate and timely action. Thus political intelligence is added to this scenario, with the result that governments must observe the international space of social media in addition to the internal policies that result in their control, because a major portion of the force applied to people movements is directed from outside the nation. However, this variable is usually uncontrollable and owing to the massive traffic volume on social media, the first point of CSMI focus is on the internal empowerment of the media and trying to control internal messages. On the other hand, how we can score the international environment and how many points we can give depend on the extent to which we have been able to control the internal environment and coordinate it with our policies. Thus for two main reasons − the need to protect the internal environment and the uncontrollability of the external environment − the focus is on the prediction of internal behaviours above all else. However, some governments regard social media intelligence as another form of traditional control. As mentioned in the previous chapter, people basically tend to take up social media in order to increase the range and quality of communications and if they feel such an environment is being controlled, they may exhibit unfavourable reactions. The Iranian government considerably extended its decision to filter the virtual environment after the unrest in 2009 and decisions such as filtering mobile-based software, including WeChat and then WhatsApp (which faced the government's opposition), were the basis of its work. On the other hand, efforts to build a national internet were another attempt to control political movements among the people as a result of governmental collapse. In fact, Iran and Saudi Arabia continue the policies of countries which have previously shown that control cannot be a useful tool for the protection of the government. It is noteworthy that all of such controls were exercised during the unrest in Iran in 2009 when, owing to the slow speed of the Internet and the filtering of social networks, such media were not actually of use as a tool to push forward a political agenda. However, they could be considered a means of external pressure on the Iranian government and so this factor and fear of global public opinion have led to the Iranian government to exercise greater control so that it can decrease internal pressures in spite of its inability to control world opinion. Overall, Iran could be viewed a successful government that, in spite of low social intelligence, is able to prohibit civic movements by other means. However, as discussed throughout this book, there have been several instances in which tools of control could not stop the people coming together. Using the experts' points of view in this book, a path was selected as the one for social media intelligence at the national level that would include the segmentation of the political market in the social media, the selection of the message, the selection of the media and the sending of the message, feedback and improvement in the process.

Political market segmentation in the social media

The first step in managing social media is to know the people who are active in the media. However, given the numbers of such people in any country, face-to-face marketing approaches can no longer be used. Even though it is said that the Internet and social media make it possible to create a better understanding of people (personal marketing), there is no opportunity to do this in times of crisis. Thus those groups with similar characteristics must be selected and accordingly be contacted instead of individuals.

Individuals and authority groups (reference groups)

If you can align yourself with individuals and groups in social networks who attract other people, the road ahead will be simpler. This is important when we recall previous chapters, where we saw that the majority of people in social networks are followers, rejecting or accepting others' opinions but not acting as leaders themselves. This is a positive point for governments wishing to direct this great energy towards their goals. Although technology has changed the views of Iranian and Arab people concerning the clergy somewhat, they can also act as authority groups. However, there is a serious problem. For instance, in Iran, the clerics simply do not take part in social networks because they have rejected technology and have fought against it; their presence in the media will therefore prompt different reactions. Hence the need for them to make changes in their views on the technology and to be present in these networks is very pressing in the networks and the issue is vital, as it could be argued that an unnecessary battle between religion and technology will lead to the destruction of theocracy. On the other hand, since the social media in Arab countries and Iran are devoid of religious and governmental forces, things have been easy for their opponents. Another point that was again neglected by governments is that it is not necessary for these authorities or nodes in social networks to be real people, but different tools can be deployed in order to become such a node. However, to what extent these people can influence others in times of crisis is unclear, and thus using the people who are influential in the real world can be associated with a higher degree of confidence. Another issue in the Arab countries and Iran is that throughout history, individualism as well as the failure of most parties has made prominent people in these countries responsible for attracting others, whereas this task is carried out by the parties themselves in many developed countries and represents another potential opportunity for forming groups and authoritative voices in social media. Any dynamic society sees a movement in groups and authority figures during its lifetime and changes in influential groups in different communities can over a period of time easily be observed, investigated and a conclusion reached whether at present the group has a positive effect on changes.

Information literacy and media literacy

As mentioned in previous chapters, a good index can predict people's behaviour in a web environment. If indicators such as literacy and or level of education were used in a traditional segmentation of the target market, the current degree of reaction to a message in social media is a direct function of people's information and media literacies. This is related to some degree to individuals' educational levels; however, there are several instances where people with little education have shown media literacy. Just as being a figure of authority attracting followers can determine people's effectiveness, media literacy can too. The relatively low levels of media literacy in the Arab countries and Iran again provide an opportunity for governments to influence the people and there will also be the threat of influence from external pressures. Since an entire chapter has been devoted to this issue and there are adequate criteria for its measurement, this issue is not discussed further in this section.

Receiving a message what happens

Let us return to the examples of global business in order to understand the importance of this index. This example aims to show that although the social media are a way to reduce the cost of access to users, even high-performance private commercial companies have made a mistake in identifying the path along which users receive messages. This can probably be linked with more mistakes, because there are fewer experts on social media directing messages from government than there are in a big global business. Results indicating this were obtained by the author of this book from other research studies on global business. In this study, first of all, messages of corporate social responsibility (CSR) published by 50 top global companies in social media were extracted and the ways in which these messages were transferred were identified (see Table 6.1).

As expected, use of the company website was the simplest means to distribute CSR messages and a majority of the companies studied employed this method. However, two popular social media networks also contributed considerably, and at least 21 companies have used Facebook for this purpose. The Twitter network, however, was apparently more popular among the companies studied and at least 23 companies used it for the publication of CSR messages. It is probable that

Table **6.1** Types of social media used for CSR communication

Social media	Percentage of corporations
Corporate website	72%
Facebook	42%
Twitter	46%
Blogging	16%
Audio	6%
Video	12%
Photo sharing	12%
Publishing	22%

companies selected a suitable tool for their objectives; however, we still cannot claim this for sure. Therefore we must show on which media the companies studied became more familiar with CSR messages, and on the other hand through which media they preferred to become familiar with companies' CSR (see Table 6.2).

It was found that customers have indeed received messages on social responsibility through instruments of the social media, though these have been used by relatively few companies. When a political crisis occurs, this gap will become more important and proper knowledge of the path for receiving messages is the gap between the survival or demise of a government. Social networks prioritise other methods in terms of the transfer rate of a message; however, rumour reduces the level of confidence in the published messages in such networks and it is probably for this reason that users do not use the network enough to receive what companies are really trying to say. This eight-month study investigated a group of 3,252 people from six Arab countries and Iran who responded to the questionnaire's items as discussed in previous chapters. The questionnaire included questions on methods by which they preferred to receive political messages from government and the political parties. It should be noted that the issue of preference was not considered in this section and probably what actually happened was different from the results of this section. Since we intended to create a plan for the future, it would be better to know the preferences of users. In this section, users had two options. For this reason, total percentages would not come to 100% and so those media that achieved less than 15% are not shown in Table 6.3.

Table 6.2 Types of social media viewed by customers for CSR messages

Social media	Percentage of customers
Corporate website	17%
Facebook	18%
Twitter	13%
Blog	27%
Audio	5%
Video	46%
Photo sharing	14%
Publishing	42%

Table 6.3 Types of social media preferred by respondents to obtain government and party messages in an electronic environment

Social media	Percentage of customers
Online news sites	71.3%
Video/audio sites	52.5%
Party/government website	49.1%
Social network sites	23.2%

As seen in Table 6.3, online news sites had the greatest priority for receiving the political news from government and parties, and the level of confidence in such sites is greater than in other sites because, unlike social networks, they have a greater percentage of rumour. What can be helpful in such news sites for governments is to create targeted news which could be directly available for sites through the government itself (and not the official journals) and direct opinion along a certain path in the long term.

Degree of virtual socialisation

This section deals with whether introvert and extrovert people can be distinguished in virtual communities. It is clear that the type of reaction to any message can be a function of the introversion or extroversion of individuals; however, there is not sufficient evidence to claim that introvert people in the real world are also introvert in the virtual world because use of the secrecy feature in the social media can remove some of the obstacles presented by introversion. In this study, we divided 637 respondents to the questionnaire, all of whom were Iranian and members of Facebook and Twitter, into four groups. All respondents had been members of these networks for one to two years (with a current account).

- First group: between 1 and 10 friends (possibly between one and ten posts and or tweets).
- Second group: between 11 and 50 friends (possibly between 11 and 50 posts and or tweets).
- Third group: between 51 and 150 friends (possibly between 51 and 151 posts and or tweets).
- Fourth group: over 150 friends and over 150 tweets.

Of the 1,831 people selected only 637 people responded to our online questionnaire (the whole period of data collection was 23 days). In fact, we tried to understand which people can be called introvert and extrovert in a virtual environment. Although the number of friends and conversations within the virtual community was low, 34% of them claimed that they had more than one account in similar virtual networks. For instance, if their main account, which was the reason for their selection as a sample in the study, was in the social network of Facebook, 34% of these people had at least another account with their name (7%), with another name (22%) or with both (5%) in the same social network. This percentage was nearly equal to 1.4% for the fourth group but there was no significance between the second and third groups. Having more accounts is usually associated with some kind of secrecy and individuals can post an opinion in one account and then post the opposite in other accounts. What was of great importance for us was their type of reaction to a positive political message and a negative political message. There was no significant difference between groups in their type of reaction to the positive and negative messages; however, over 38% of individuals in both the third and fourth groups shared their messages and/or gave a comment on them. Content analysis of these comments indicated that the reaction to such messages was logical and only a few of them responded beyond the pale to the messages.

Similarly, in the first group, nearly 29% of individuals posted comments and a few also shared messages. However, content analysis of the messages in many cases (nearly half) indicated some type of agitation or extreme behaviour. Whether participants of the study are called introvert or extrovert, the results showed that those receiving the political messages must be classified according to the degree of action and reaction in the virtual environment so that appropriate messages can be designed for each group.

The producer or consumer of the content?

The experts in our study prioritised the factor of content production as the second important index of segmentation after the reference people and groups. They believed that a small number of people produced an important part of the content in the social networks and media. In order to prove the claim, 1,000 personal pages were closely investigated at random from only six countries in the Twitter network, that is, five Arab countries and Iran. The number of tweets (minus retweets) was important for the study. The investigation of the content showed that about 0.73% of these tweets belonged to 0.19% of users and 14 people out of the total 0.19% could be classified as popular, while others were ordinary. This indicated that people with greater content are a small part of the community in the social media. It should be noted that those producing content should not be confused with reference people or groups because a reference person or group may not produce a lot of content and only be selected as a reference because of their fame or popularity. Thus, if the content producers are considered to be a market segment and the consumers of that content as another sector, were governments to focus on the investment in content producers they would take a majority of the market. Again, note that if the government can attract to their side in this case the maximum or at best 0.19% of users who are producing content, the whole community in fact is under control and the cultural concerns of the government will significantly decline (although that 0.19% seems almost impossible to control). Let us look at the issue from another angle. In Iran and the Arab countries being studied, more than half of the families in the country are dependent on the government (although they may not ideologically agree with that system) owing to the fact that the government keeps all personal affairs under constant surveillance and the private sector is not as active as in developed countries. Iran's government, encourages government personnel to be present at important religious and civil ceremonies, so the same personnel must become content producers. This requires continuous training, but at least it is better than the overthrow of the government. What the experts involved in the study insisted upon was to create cultural content and try to preserve the culture of the people. They believed that maintaining cultural roots might prove an obstacle to the collapse of the state. However, when a home-grown technology competes at the local level over time and the community gradually becomes familiar with its different aspects, it prepares itself for the correct use of the technology. In contrast, when a state is a long way from the use of important knowledge and modern technology that appear so exciting for young people with regard to their communication capabilities, the development of such technology is achieved at great speed owing to the excessive increase in demand. In practice, it is a shock to the community while people are not still ready to digest and deal properly with the technology. As seen earlier, a majority of the users in Arab countries joined the social network in a very short time, which became the reason for the lack of culture creation, and many people did not give the government a chance. However, Iran and Saudi Arabia have successfully weathered the storm in the region and now have the opportunity for cultural creation and the production of healthy content in order to change public opinion. We might think of the Internet as a cultural pathway leading to a change in the culture in two ways. First, any technology basically has a culture with respect to its origin by which the culture transfers, such as the culture of open communications or the presence of critics in the social networks. Secondly, such a technology is a confluence of different cultures, in which the cultures change each other and the dominant culture will contain a set of the features of all cultures in it and will partly retain its root characteristics. However, how do we try to become the dominant culture? In our study, two factors — language and trust — account for the most important of the barriers to the cultural development of Arab countries and Iran. On the one hand, the language used in such countries, that is Persian and Arabic, is not the dominant language in social media. Therefore cultural products can cross those countries' borders, but it may not be possible to penetrate the international market. On the other hand, trust in the news issued by the internal media of these countries is very low and people prefer to receive necessary content from British social media. This results in some difficulties in producing content for the government. Thus, the first step to promote the production of national content is to build trust in the content produced by the internal media and also to produce the content in an international language so that, in addition to the influence of other cultures, the internal culture can be affected by the content produced. Other factors, such as national identity, can also be seen to segment the political market. However, as this has been dealt with in a previous chapter, we will not consider it again here.

Message design, media selection and message sending

The selection and building of a message are closely related to the features of content production and must be conducted according to the knowledge of the user. Indeed, a certain message must be transferred after the market segmentation according to the characteristics of each part of the market, in order to achieve greater effectiveness. Today, a lack of a strategic plan for content production, a lack of familiarity with the basic structure of social media or understanding of the audience, a lack of trained and specialised manpower, a lack of thought regarding content production and a mismatch between the content generated and a particular media are the major problems for governments to produce a message appropriate to the characteristics of the target community. Recently, both political and commercial campaigns have produced only single-channel content, which is also one of the factors accelerating the demise of Arab regimes. Thus, in the case of a multi-channel viewpoint and particularly the content production for any particular channel, the trend was definitely in another direction. Today, the method of making the best content to achieve the maximum results – called content marketing – is noted. Here, we intend to express its characteristics in political marketing, which is different from the marketing of goods and services. Such marketing is an appropriate instrument to raise the information and media literacy indices of the people. In fact, it eliminates competitors in apparently scientific terms and strengthens our political campaign. On the other hand, since we promoted the target market literacy, the potential and actual users and beneficiaries of this government or political party will have a higher loyalty to it.

What have we done?

The first content that a government or party must attend to is to use the principles of no deception and express the facts. Although we may try to gather advocates for ourselves through deception and illusion, the activities conducted must first be emphasised. What we have done so far can be transmitted to the people in several ways, such as infographics. Attempts to improve lives, welfare, education, health and so forth can be provided for the public in a comprehensive and fascinating overview. This kind of message must put greater emphasis on the dimensions of transfer rate and attractiveness, because the first step must be a very powerful one. Media such as photo sharing and YouTube, and even publishing media such as wikis have a good effect in this case.

What have others done?

This section emphasises the comparative analysis of the activities carried out by the government or party and previous governments, and the inputs and outputs are compared to each other. We will try to highlight the negative points of government opposition and parties that can be illustrated by infographics. If a new emerging party has been set up before us with no previous record (which, for example, has been much the case in Egypt where new parties have been formed), so that its negative points or weaknesses could not be highlighted, our advertising slogans and strategies must be focused on what potential negative consequences of their strategies can be expected. An important point that must be stressed here is to use people's previous experiences. For instance, an unpleasant historical event must be indirectly evoked for the people and related to the competitors' strategies, so that the people understand, if they support the competitor party, that such an event may happen again. When this message is provided for the people through a social media network, via a reference person or group, its effect could be doubled because the believability of that message will be increased. People trust that reference person or group, thus their message will be trusted.

The innovative content and generator of core identity

After the Iranian elections and resultant public unrest in 2009, what the group of reformers had as their winning ticket was the creation of a common identity. Thus all supporters of the reformers recognised their identity (liberal and intellectual); and such shared identity made them more coherent, so that a serious move against the government was made for the first time since 1979.This discussion is completely different from that on national identity that was mentioned in Chapter 2, and its objective was to create coherence of thought. If governments can create a coherent identity through social media, they can guide the people's thoughts in critical circumstances as necessary. In cyberspace and in the age of globalisation, since access to information and communication is easier and faster than ever before, citizens who enter cyberspace have a greater basic tendency to get information and enjoy greater knowledge, and have incremental demands in the expectation of participating in the public affairs of their community. Governments can use this as an opportunity for an optimal and low-cost solution to several problems that have been encountered. One-dimensional orientations and inclinations are the methods that political parties in Egypt adopted after the revolution, and were then a sign of extremism and that they could not understand the phenomena and dynamic processes of identity and do not properly understand the value of different interests and tastes. On the contrary, policy and logical process based on the identity policy-makers' feedback and the avoidance of destructive, exclusive and extreme attitudes and behaviours can be a sensible strategy to balance multiple and diverse identities. Such identity strategy has the ability to reduce stresses and conflicts effectively. When our politics content is partly based on user-generated content, it means that all requirements are seen in it and are based in continuous learning. Social networks have the most effect in content production. It is natural that the creation of a quiet environment with mutual understanding results in optimal and low-cost identity policies. However, when can such moderation can be created in identity politics?

The shareable content with prestige

Consider the Twitter page of the US president Barack Obama (*@BarackObama*). In addition to more than one link, most tweets make use of a lot of pictures and videos. Now look at the number of retweets. You can see that the reputation of a person such as Obama has much more power for transmitting messages. It means that a message that was issued by him once will be shared thousands of times by other viewers. Note that the retweet of a message does not mean the viewer is in absolute agreement and you may even make the decision to retweet that message in spite of disagreeing with it. Sometimes a retweet may be so that our followers know we are also followers of Barack Obama's page. This creates some type of prestige for us. Note too this fine point, that the creation of prestige for content leads to an increase in the number of retweets. Just as buying a luxury car created prestige in the past, nowadays being a follower or doing a retweet can create prestige for some people. However, it is clear that following a person such as Obama, who is the most powerful politician in the world, differs from following a party or government in Arab and Middle Eastern countries. Our expert team believes that the young population in the Arab countries and Iran often share messages that are signs of their intellectuality; however, this requires more research in the future.

Content that creates engagement

Many Arab and Middle Eastern countries enjoy a seemingly unlimited wealth of natural resources and oil. The question raised by the people in such countries, however, is, how are these resources allocated? Why is the living standard very low in many countries in spite of their rich resources, and why is the class gap greater than in developed countries? By using social media, budget preferences can be selected in consultation with the people, and the people's trust in the government will be increased. However, imagine that you are in a community where there is no political participation to date and you understand that you could unwittingly have a major role in government decisions. It is clear that such participation cannot have a positive result, owing to the lack of political knowledge among the citizens. The first step, then, is to build an infrastructure and educational content for the people. Most often, citizens do not have a good understanding of what participation entails, that is, they do not know what advantages participation will bring for them and how participation will affect their future. On the other hand, people in third-world countries have difficulty with corporate communication and unlike individual behaviours, collaborative behaviours are always difficult to teach. Many people consider themselves either superior or inferior to others and so they do not have enough incentive to participate. Therefore the creation of uniformity, which is the most important feature of the collaborative communication, will be very difficult. In fact, it can be argued that one reason for the lack of political participation in social media is insufficient awareness, a problem which education can overcome for governments. The degree of political and social awareness among the citizens has a direct relationship to the degree and quality of information flow, ease of access to it and public trust in information resources. In general, the people's party or team, their business, social and political tendencies and their reaction to the government's performance in political, social and economic arenas depend on background awareness. As a result, content that can be synchronously informative can also improve political engagement in the long term and achieve governmental objectives with a lower cost.

Content creating legitimacy

In addition to what was stated in the previous chapters on legitimacy and the legitimacy crisis, it must be said that legitimacy can be observed in the content when the principles of good governance can be introduced to the people on the Internet. The World Bank presented several indices for this situation. Here, we will describe some examples of indicators that can be strengthened by the capabilities of social media. Voice and accountability are among these indices. This means that people can query and prosecute the government about what influences them. This index includes concepts such as political rights, freedom of expression, sociopolitical assemblies, freedom of the press, the number of representative rulers of social classes, political processes in elections, and so forth. During the people's movements in the Arab countries and even in Iran, many of the political rallies were coordinated through the Internet. However, the government always called such assemblies unauthorised and tried to prevent them from taking place, giving rise to violence in the assemblies (and a reduction in the legitimacy of government). On the other hand, government agreement with an assembly on social media and even the presence of government representatives in such assemblies could result in peaceful public gatherings. In fact, governments have the opportunity through social media to predict people's movements before they begin and they can also attend their meetings in order to respond to the people so that people trust them more than ever. The presentation of satisfactory content to the people so that they know they have the right to hold gatherings and express opinions freely at any time can induce good governance in people's minds as well. For example, in Iran, after the adoption of the filtering of some mobile-based applications, the government of President Rouhani opposed this development. This caused an increase in public confidence for the government as a result of its support for freedom in the virtual environment, an issue that had enormous benefits at low cost for Iran. Moreover, the use of strategies to reduce poverty through information technology can greatly decrease the possibility of revolution in search of equality and justice, with improvement in the people's welfare. Naturally, in order to increase efficiency in the process of empowerment of the poor, it is necessary first to produce practical and appropriate content for them, and secondly to introduce training to use the content generated. Thus, the basic rule is to create enabling content, so that any person can become a potential entrepreneur with sufficient free training. Thus both educational poverty and economic poverty are alleviated. In fact, IT application is an economic, cultural and social phenomenon. On the one hand it requires cultural, social, economic and political contexts while on the other hand, as an active factor, it can influence cultural and social behaviours and relations at the community level. This phenomenon can also result in some innovation and transformation in people's attitudes. Although such transformations are necessary for any development, they have existed throughout history and may have destructive effects as well. As the most important emerging phenomenon, IT has a concrete role in the development of other technologies and has a profound effect on social and cultural infrastructures. For this reason, the introduction of every manifestation of IT into society involves recognition of its cultural outcomes and planning to bring it to a local level. This means that the Arab countries and Iran, which always emphasise copying Western education for their citizens and make no investment in the production of local content, will have no choice but the destruction of what they have built and cannot build legitimacy for themselves. It is clear that if the content of such technology can be brought to the local level and then internalised, problems in the cultural and social fields can also be solved. However, if you look at it simply from a technological and hardware point of view, there are many problems in the application and interaction. For example, the spread of the Internet in the nations of the Middle

East should occur in a way that contributes to the development of creativity and does not result in a retrograde step. Policy on the development of the Internet should not be limited to expanding its consumption or reproducing its content but must extend to the development of native and religious culture and cultural resistance so as to establish enough legitimacy for the governments of the Middle Eastern region. The researcher believes that we need powerful internal social networks to create legitimate content before anything else in order to guide the people in crisis situations by producing enough trust. Iran has been making attempts to address this issue and, for instance, has created the Aparat.com website, a video-sharing service to replace YouTube, the Irexpert.ir site, a social expert network to replace Linkedin, and the Cloob.com network instead of global social networks such as Facebook. Although these sites are not as popular as the global sites, they are steps in the right direction in themselves and can have a positive impact on people's minds.

Feedback and improvement on the message

In many countries, the use of information technology and social media to connect with people is only a one-way process to transfer messages to the people. However, the most important feature of social media, which is to get feedback using user-generated content, is forgotten. This will lead to a poor view of the state social media among the people. Arguably, it can be said that perhaps the most difficult of the steps outlined in this chapter is this section, on message feedback and improvement, because the ways of giving feedback from the public to a government in social media are so various and wide-ranging that they cannot be quantified. One person may give his feedback by sharing a video on YouTube, while another gives it by writing a short text in a blog or a comment on a news site. Thus what will be helpful in this case is content analysis, and theme analysis in some cases. Clearly, a large amount of feedback from users can be an opportunity to survive the regime or a threat to destroy it. When the feedback is met with an appropriate response, the chance of survival is extended. Hence, the first step is to identify the feedback and then respond to it. There are obviously several methods and software applications to analyse large amounts of data and we do not aim to introduce them in this section of the book. However, some practical techniques are discussed below.

Create a platform specific for the people's feedback on social media

A special way to pass on feedback specific to the voice of the people should be created. You do not need to seek public feedback on all sites and social media, but they are the people who will come to you with feedback. If this platform allows you to share images, video, text and so forth, it will be easier to analyse its content so that the people's needs are quickly investigated and the roots of the matter are detected. In addition, the rate of responsiveness is reduced. It is the factor by which governments can benefit principally in a crisis situation because people's patience has no meaning in such circumstances. We should recognise that the response to feedback can avert thousands or even millions of other negative feedback postings while no response to feedback can result in the beginning of a revolution. Such civil movement is a kind of political engagement. However, remember that in this case, not only will it not reduce the importance of content analysis but also, having a very strong political-content analysis team can reveal the true capabilities of the platform.

Be a learning government

You are probably familiar with the concept of a learning organisation, a concept which, if ignored or not understood, could lead to the organisation's demise at the hands of competitors. Earlier, we talked about the importance of learning to users, but learning within the state can be even more important. The boundaries of traditional hierarchies of authority must be broken down to move towards a learner government. In traditional states, senior officials who are responsible for leading and recognising the strategies of government are obliged to think and act for the entire government. People just play the role of voters and intellectual supporters of the government. However, in a horizontal state, which is created via the benefits of using information technology, people are given more authority and trial and error will be based on people's needs. Today, the old adage 'knowledge is power' cannot be applied everywhere, but at the root of this knowledge in a learner government is communications. Proper communication is the source of government power, and could lead to the production or updating of knowledge. Before its introduction into social media it represented implicit knowledge for the government, and now it has been transformed into explicit knowledge. However, it should be noted that the difficulty in understanding implicit knowledge is not a barrier for its transfer to the government. For this reason, mutual cooperation between the government and the public and a long-term relationship between the two can transfer this knowledge.

Provide motivation for feedback

According to the results of a study (in the physical environment of Iran and not in the virtual environment), only 26% of respondents gave comments on government performance in the social media, generated content and comments and shared photos and videos in the case of agreement or disagreement with government activities. It is notable that only 3% of all respondents also considered giving solutions and suggestions. However, 79% of respondents continually talk about government activities and performance with others in their daily lives. We can see that there is a huge gap between individuals who just talk with others, those who leave a message on social media and those who give solutions. It means that given the pervasiveness of social media, we have been able to find scattered information on the comments of only 26% of people. The other 74% either do not talk about the government and politics, or just talk about it informally without being registered somewhere. This could amount to a huge force during a crisis situation and no government would be able to meet their needs. Therefore motivation to give feedback on the government and its workings will be a fundamental principle. So far, we have found how to create a platform and use knowledge and learning concepts but our data and inputs do not represent the entire community's view. Thus the gap must be filled in somehow. The first motivation for giving feedback is that people know their feedback receives attention and is addressed as soon possible. Therefore, showing that the government has an option to resolve problems posed by your feedback can be a great motivation for political participation. However, it is not possible to fully implement a process for responding to the feedback and in such a situation governments must provide logical reasons why all these problems cannot be solved. For instance, they must understand that, say, three years' effort is needed to resolve a particular problem with the resources to hand, but if the people engage in this effort the result will be achieved faster. In this case, people will peacefully follow government activities without disruption and on the other hand will engage in solving the problem and become an executive arm of the government. Furthermore, political crowdsourcing can be very useful, so as to hear the opinions of different people on how to proceed, because their ideas for a solution result from their knowledge of the roots of the problem. As it is the people who always have to cope with such problems, they are better able to get to the bottom of the problems and suggest better solutions to government. When the problems and innovative ideas are expressed in depth and are of a high quality, governments will inevitably change their procedures. There is no doubt that the Wikileaks site will cause changes in the foreign policy of many countries around the world with respect to America and may improve information security in many. If every citizen took the view that the comments in his or her feedback may bring about a change in policy, every citizen can be a part of Wikileaks, even when the amount of feedback is at its lowest level. The above-mentioned issues imply that being an 'electronic' government cannot be considered an advantage for the government alone, but given the great number of people in the online environment, the people and their opinions should be classified and a special message written for them or a special message received from them in accordance with their needs. In this way, we can see the best electronic monitoring. It should be noted that electronic monitoring is one of the central elements and levers of e-government and not the entirety of e-government. In other words, electronic monitoring alone does not work, but is a means to improve and promote other government services which monitor government agencies, the reduction in degeneration and the feedback received from the public. In this chapter the author has tried to emphasise some of the issues of political marketing in the virtual world. In political systems, competition among the political actors who are aiming to gain power or influence decisions within the parties depends largely on the quality of the marketing of themselves and political, public and social activities against public thoughts. Political marketing is considered only as a fixed point in developing countries, in Iran and in countries in the Middle East. Political marketing activities start three to five months before an election and end after the elections finish, although in a country like America, for instance, this process is always rolling forward and is scheduled long before the election. Interestingly, the fixed-point method would usually be effective in the Middle East for political marketing activities and many of the political marketing rules would have basically the opposite result in these countries. This can be caused by many of the indices mentioned in the previous chapters, that is the excitement of people, the heavy dependence on people to meet primary economic needs, the level of media and information literacy, the level of trust between government and people, social capital and legitimacy. If the political systems of these countries really operate in terms of the long-term development of their country and not just winning the election and taking power temporarily, they must know that they are responsible for one of the most important tasks, that is to enhance the political awareness and literacy level of the people so that successful policy models of the developed countries can be founded within them locally in the long term. Thus the third world could become a rich sector, like the countries on the margins of the Persian Gulf, to give the most optimistic scenario. Otherwise, they will never develop intellectually and politically, despite having such wealth, and will have only a developed appearance, with a rotten and dependent interior.

References

Thorndike, E. (1920). Intelligence and its uses. *Harper's Monthly Magazine, 140,* 227–235.
Wawra, D. (2009). Social intelligence: the key to intercultural communication. *European Journal of English Studies, 13*(2), 163–177.

Further reading

Aitamurto, T. (2012). *Crowdsourcing for democracy: a new era in policy-making.* Available at: <http://web.eduskunta.fi/dman/Document.phx?documentId = aj31112105519943>.
Bott, M., & Young, G. (2012). *The role of crowdsourcing for better governance in international development.* Available at: <http://fletcher.tufts.edu/praxis/ ~ /media/Fletcher/Microsites/praxis/xxvii/4BottYoungCrowdsourcing.pdf>.

Strategic analysis and future strategies

Introduction

This chapter is a comprehensive study investigating the influence of internal and external forces acting on social media penetration to enhance democracy and social justice and design strategies for them. A common problem in strategic management is that the strategy is designed without a clear goal. During strategic analysis of a country or organisation, for example, the question is asked, what internal and external forces are affecting the organisation? This conversation is basically misguided, because when the strategic analysis and diagnosis of internal and external forces is carried out, for example with a focus on democracy and justice, the result may be quite different from the original purpose, for example, creating good relationships with neighbouring countries. The fundamental objectives of the revolutions in the Arab countries and Iran were democracy and social justice, with the main areas discussed in this book as they arise.

The goal of our strategic analysis, based on the objectives of social media penetration to promote democracy and social justice, was developed in the Middle East. It should be noted that the strategies proposed in this chapter can also be used for people as protestors as well as by governments in the region to restore peace to the people. So we tried to design final strategies with multiple objectives. Rapidly increasing changes in information technology in the fields of hardware, software, application systems and networks have led to a short-term overall view; however, there are not the skills necessary for the proper utilisation of ICT.

Since ICT is changing rapidly, a very large programme of analysis away from the details to determine the way to direct the movement of society towards information technology is urgently needed. The problem is solved with the strategic analysis of information technology. To begin the process, a PESTEL analysis of the environment is selected, including the political, economic, social, technological, legal and environmental factors of the participants in this study. Owing to a lack of proper environmental analysis for social media, ethical analysis is used instead. This is a requirement-oriented analysis to prevent useless strategies. One very important point that should be mentioned is that, since we have examined in this analysis only the weaknesses and threats, it is not a complete analysis. However, its aims are to demonstrate that the social media penetration barriers to the promotion of democracy and social justice to policy-makers in each country can improve their situation, depending on their policies. These barriers are most common in the countries examined but because they vary so greatly in terms of their strengths, the full analysis is beyond this discussion.

Online Arab Spring.

Analysis of political factors

The first political factor that can be a barrier to social media penetration to promote democracy and social justice is government instability, and more importantly the uncertainty of the laws enacted by the government. There are many examples of this in the Middle East, where good laws relating to information technology were passed in a given country but for various reasons, such as a change of government or even the absence of sufficient force, reached a dead end. (This could also be included in the legal factors, but according to the experts, because of its roots in political instability, it should be in this section. One of the main reasons for this instability is that the countries studied here have been caught between two internal forces. On the one hand, one force has a tendency to rapid progression by adopting laws from advanced countries while on the other hand, the other force tends to regulate the situation through internal capabilities and support from their national culture and customs.

So every group that comes to power in a country is accompanied by policies to change previous laws. One group may understand social media penetration as a way to increase communication with the outside world while a second group may view it as endangering the stability of the country. Mediocrity is usually caused by the same factors – lack of proper use of social media by the people and the use of illegal practices such as anti-filters to access social media. Obviously, in this case, even entering a social media network is an illegal act that is not subject to proper policies to optimise their use. The next factor is the multi-curator of the IT field in Middle Eastern countries. While experts in the field of IT are to be found in advanced countries, this field has several curators in the Middle East. While on the one hand huge issues may be dealt within the Ministry of Information and Communications Technology, on the other hand important issues are also dealt with in the various cultural ministries. More interestingly, rather than each ministry itself making decisions in the field of information technology separately, such decisions come from people who do not have any expertise in this area.

Therefore, the lack of specialisation and the absence of a single person in charge of macro policy are the major obstacles to the use of social media for creating social justice. Everything falls under the banner of IT policy basically, except for social justice and democracy. If we take Iran, there are numerous institutions in charge of information technology, which is one of the major problems that impedes the development of this technology in Iran. The Supreme Council of Information, the Supreme Council of Technology Information, the Supreme Council of Informatics, the Development Center of Information Technology and Digital Media of the Ministry of Culture and Islamic Guidance, the Information and Communication Technology Management and Security Committee, the Deputy President for Science and Technology, the Ministry of Science, Research and Technology and several other institutions and organisations are involved in the planning and guiding of IT. The multiplicity of actors and their parallel and sometimes overlapping missions is one of the serious problems in the development of IT in Iran. Perhaps only in the areas of education and health is the use of information technology (not social media) leading to the promotion of justice. However, a large part of this was not due to policy but arose from the natural advantages to be had from IT transferred into this sector.

The next factor to be discussed is a combination of sanctions and lack of the political will among the countries of the West to bring democracy and justice to the countries of the Middle East. A large proportion of the world's wealth of natural resources lies in the countries of the Middle East. The creation of social justice and democracy in these countries will mean that developed countries will be in need of energy and access to these resources will be more difficult. This is not so good for advanced countries, who can create chaos in these countries, keeping them in poverty with fighting between the government and the people, and thus acquire the the resources much more cheaply. Social media sources have also been created in developed countries, where the penetration strategies of the media for creating democracy and justice is well known, so that they can more easily access cheap resources.

In fact there is an indirect sanction in these countries, such that even with the correct policy the desired results may not be achieved. Approaches based on this scenario should be designed to achieve the best results. The next factor could be a named security policy. Media such as YouTube can be seen as weapons in the fight against the governments of the Middle East by the people and many videos about violations of the law by the government, corruption in governments, etc. are shared. In fact, people have tried to show how the authorities have banned such items. The result is that these media increase access by the general public to information about the government and the ruling elite which could jeopardise national security. Thus policies have been adopted in order to reduce public access to the tools, rather than to extend the goals of democracy and justice. When a government has a full vote of confidence from the media in its country having adopted the right approach, it should not worry about the exposure of illegal activities.

The problem of the lack of suitable technology in relevant government agencies is also noted. As Bayo-Moriones and Lera-Lopez (2007) note, IT adoption by other users on the network can have a positive influence on the technology adopted by companies in that sector. Since e-government programmes often have a synergistic aspect, sectors such as government departments, the private sector, NGOs and citizens acting as key stakeholders are brought together and involved in this type of IT application (Potnis, 2010). Thus the absence of such programmes in one part of the chain, in addition to the backwardness of the state, leads to failure to engage industry and the private sector.

Analysis of economic factors

The creation of powerful social media that can compete internationally requires an initial investment, in some cases by venture capitalists (VCs) in developed countries on the one hand, while on the other hand the rich experience of the management of those media will also be required. However, the weakness or even absence of investment companies that invest in the IT sector is one of the most important economic problems. The IT industry and health care have always been of interest to the venture capitalist because, if taken up at the appropriate stage, companies can make profits several times greater than the initial investment for executives and groups. With the lack of a national system of innovation or a university system that encourages creativity and entrepreneurship, the lack of entrepreneurship education in the development of a new industry, the lack of investors to invest in businesses that are high-risk and high-yield, the reluctance of foreign investors owing to the lack of security for foreign investment, the lack of state funds for research and technology, one of the pillars of its activities – to raise capital for the venture – including the provision of economic problems in the field of IT, will be blocked. One aspect of the weakness is the return to political instability in which firms tend not to invest in IT in the Middle East while another consists of the government's influence in the field of investment. Middle Eastern governments are willing to invest in these key profitable areas and provide their own security. Once again the need for democracy and justice in policy has been abandoned. Here we look at the sanctions on Iran which could be an appropriate model for other Arab countries. Economic sanctions always have both positive and negative impacts.

On the one hand, sanctions have particularly unpleasant consequences for Iran's industry and also specifically for IT in Iran's industry. The most important companies providing software packages are not willing to cooperate with Iranian companies because of the political and economic sanctions. However, this situation appears to challenge only the largest and most important Iranian companies, because only large companies could be clients for software packages and services that support them. However, if we look at models of the spread of technology, it becomes clear that this situation would affect the whole industry. On the other hand, the national infrastructure and the international sanctions boost self-sufficiency in the production of knowledge related to IT, and the growing number of IT professionals in the country with transnational power is self-evident.

Analysis of social factors

This analysis has had its remit in the social and cultural spheres. As mentioned in previous chapters, to some extent, in the countries of the Middle East, the wave of social media technology did not come about by incremental improvements, but arrived quite suddenly, so there was no time to develop a technological culture. The great potential of social media for people to express thoughts freely and yet remain hidden behind a changed identity has led to many people living under oppression enjoying only one of the benefits of a social media, while being unable to enjoy all of their applications.

An interesting discovery of our research is that, at the lower level of media literacy, if you are confronted with a message or photo that does not correspond with reality but seems professional and is designed to look good, most likely it will elicit a 'Like' or a comment or be shared. An attack launched in this way may appear very simple, but such details can lead to catastrophe and gradually the negative message becomes a wave. What could this mean in such a volatile situation? Where will justice and democracy, be in people's awareness? After the promotion of culture, technology and media literacy in the Middle East, countries in the region are faced with numerous constraints, one of the biggest obstacles being the difficulty in establishing justice and democracy through social media. On the other hand, with a young and promising workforce in these countries with some education, these problems cannot be prevented from the outset. Education in the field of information technology and computers in these countries is not lacking, but until the social media world is recognised for its true value, education can easily be placed in the service of government policies. The next factor has to be sought in the cultural industries of Middle Eastern countries. Efforts were made in industries such as book publishing and literature on the one hand, rather than the discovery and output of knowledge, while the translation of Western scientific idolatry led to the rapid penetration of Western culture into the country. On the other hand, the absence of adequate copyright laws resulted in the loss of good ideas in these turbulent countries. You can also see in the traditions of family roots in Middle Eastern countries that these societies attach great value to families, while a fear of technology and social media is also to be observed. It cannot be said with certainty that this is an issue of weakness or strength. The traditional family of Middle Eastern countries recognises social media and information technology as factors in the entertainment of young people, while relationships are built with the opposite sex out of wedlock and children are separated from the family. As mentioned earlier, on the one hand, governments are afraid of technology because it could lead to corruption, while on the other hand some people are afraid of technology and find it difficult to access areas of democracy and justice through it.

Analysis of technological and technical factors

All the factors previously listed basically suggest that current governments are reluctant to develop infrastructure in the the countries of the Middle East. Comparing the speed of the Internet in Middle Eastern countries with the global average shows that there is much room for improvement. It should be carefully noted that the rate of growth of the IT infrastructure in Middle Eastern countries is very fast but nevertheless is lower than the global average. To analyse the technological factors, the preparation model Readiness, Activity, Impact (RAI) can be used. Indicators and topics of interest in the use of IT in selected industries are organised according to preparation model and activity. Based on this model, IT publications can be found in the three layers of fitness, activity and effectiveness of a company or industry, while the overall system is studied and assessed. The three layers are discussed below.

Readiness

The layers in the review of IT publishing or social media indicate the availability of the technical infrastructure, business and social needs and the development of skills related to this technology in human resources applied in the industry (Ghazinouri Naeini and Tavakol, 2011).

Perhaps only in human resources in the Middle Eastern countries is staffing capacity adequate, but where matters such as e-commerce and the use of social media for business are concerned, there are many shortcomings. There is still not a huge number of Internet-based businesses in Middle Eastern countries. Suppose you use social media to promote your business, the occasional lack of access to the Internet and the filtering of useful websites and even e-mail services can do nothing but harm your activities. Obviously, despite the insecurity, you might well prefer traditional commerce.

Activity

This overall index reflects the use of IT in industry as investigated. In the activity index, the success of the activity is not considered, but the strength and frequency of the activities carried out in the context of the deployment of IT, regardless of the effect of the technology, whether expected or not, are (Ghazinouri Naeini and Tavakol, 2011). Owing to the strong filtering in the Middle East countries, heavy use of social media in business development is extremely weak. Globally, more than sixty per cent of top companies have at least each a personal page on Facebook or Twitter, but according to our study of the Middle Eastern countries, this percentage is on average 15 to 20%, while in Iran it is 2%.

Impact

The final layer of the review of IT publishing shows the results of the activities carried out in the use of this technology (Ghazinouri Naeini and Tavakol, 2011), which does not fit into this discussion. In addition to the technical infrastructure, the social media content and intellectual infrastructure should also be noted, as mentioned in the previous chapter. Owing to deficiencies in the technical infrastructure, the social media content infrastructure is also not considered. Care must be taken to ensure that the state cannot become the most important producers of content in social media because factors such as the volume of activity will demand other means to use the power of the people. Mainly owing to the low media literacy in communities, and production of content that is second-hand or very poorly done, the quality of the media needs to be improved. However, in the long term it will be troublesome for democracy and justice because, instead of expressing real intentions in the media, writing and producing content only for the short term is taking a weak role in the media.

Analysis of legal factors

Laws related to privacy in social media are among the weaknesses of Middle Eastern countries, even though responsibilities in this area have been identified for government agencies. Because entry into social media takes place through illegal or proxy means, when privacy is violated in this environment it is easy to find the culprit. In many cases the affected person even prefers not to complain because only a small percentage of the complaints are likely to achieve results. Because of this, in Middle Eastern countries there are examples of both good and bad social media. Media controlled by the government are good media, even if there are infringements of privacy, but media not controlled by the state are bad. However, we must realise that it is in the nature of the Internet and social media that even with detailed rules privacy can never be assured, although clear guidelines could be used to moderate the situation.

As Rashidirad, Elahi and Hasanzadeh (2009) suggest, the political/legal constraints, including those related to data streams in communications and other items, have direct and indirect impacts on areas related to information systems. On the one hand, actions and decisions to greatly increase user numbers and their capabilities are part of the main infrastructure of IT applications. On the other hand, the main use of applications such as e-commerce may be damaged owing to unreliable service and the lack of interest or willingness in managers to establish procedures to alleviate this. Such restrictions should always be considered for as long as necessary, as the use of information technology is not well rooted in the community. There have been many positive effects as well, and enough awareness among managers has been created about the benefits of using information technology in organisational processes, an impact that could be very important in maximising the use of this technology.

Analysis of ethical factors

In much of the research on social media, discussion of ethical factors is impeded by a lack of sufficient information and in some cases issues regarding copyright law and morality are raised. But given the difference in objective analysis, here we try to look at it from another angle. When can we expect to see real people with real faces promoting democracy and social justice from social media? Ethical issues in social media begin when a virtual identity is shaped and the user is able to create a picture of him- or herself as he or she would like to be, not what he or she really is. It becomes extreme when people in the real world cannot show themselves as they really are, while if they express their true opinions they face penalties that are more likely to be found in dictatorial regimes. Please re-read the previous sentence. From this statement we can clearly see that an unblemished environment and observing the ethics of social media are the effect of freedom and justice in the physical environment. It can upset all the equations, even when there has been heavy investment in social media, and we cannot obtain the desired result because of the problems in the physical environment. In this case it is better to revisit the examples of our listed companies. When a company invests a lot in their brand on social media but the employees in the organisation are not happy, the employees simply share their disastisfaction and the problems they have with the work on their personal pages on social networks.

There must be a better way than this to eliminate problems. Using the network to communicate directly with the government and the people can be useful before people share their dissatisfaction with the government, whether as themselves or under a false identity, on the public network. This is a safety valve to prevent an overflow of people's grievances. The next thing that has become clear during our research is that when a group of people who believe that social media have taken steps toward achieving their goals, the ethical points have peaked, but if the team feels that social media are phenomena that are harmful to them and which in the long term will weaken the group, failure to take note of the ethics and social media gossip from the group can eventually turn the tide in their favour. The most important points evident here are that the beginnings of such failure to comply with the ethics of such groups not only arise from social media but also from the physical environment. Suppose a religious group is strongly dissatisfied with the development of an anti-religious culture in the social media and do not see a way to deal with it. So gossip in the physical environment against social media represents attempts to blacken the reputation of social media and reduce their role in society. However, experience has shown that gossip does not end with the physical environment but evolves. The next step is for the group to create multiple pages, blogs and websites, opening up a new front in the struggle against the social media. And in the third stage of evolution, this group finds that social media must be confronted by other social media, for success to be achieved. The next thing that is one of the positive aspects of social media in the area of ethics and social justice is the high percentage of respondents who believe that regardless of whether or not governments have a role in the distribution of wealth and social justice, people must exert pressure through the Internet and social media to create justice. The minimum amount of work that must be done in this area is helping people who have low incomes and live in poverty. In all the Arab countries surveyed and Iran over 55% of people are in this situation, while the percentage in America is 38%. Most of the former are in Iran and Tunisia, at 69% and 68% per cent, respectively. This creates a strong potential for governments to increase people's capacity to take advantage of democracy and social justice, while it appears that in some Western countries, this is more of a burden on the state.

Given the importance of ethical issues and social responsibility in the virtual environment, the researcher came up with the idea of seeking new criteria for ranking websites and social media pages. Alexa.com provides website ratings in terms of the number of visits, which is a factor that has an important role in the value of a web page or website. There will be a greater need to value sites in terms of ethical standards. That is why, in the middle of 2014, an elite group of programmers in the web field came together to launch the site http://www.ethicsRank.com, and readers of this book can also assist in measuring the observance of ethics on the web. According to our investigation, the principal costs of material and moral wrongdoing in virtual space in the Middle East and developing countries are higher than in developed countries. Owing to the nature of governments in the Middle East and the need for the constant monitoring of virtual environments to counter threats, Middle Eastern countries have defined more crimes in cyberspace and consequently there is greater punishment. This can be useful, leading to a reduction in non-compliance with ethics, but it also leads to changes in the identity of most people in the virtual community and therefore it becomes uncontrollable.

Strategies for the future

The first and perhaps most important strategy for social media policy in the Middle East is standardisation. There is a general requirement for broad decision-making in this field, as well as specific standards for the respective ministries to begin to use information technology and social media. When a ministry has been willing to make extensive changes to goals and procedures, this has always had a good outcome in terms of policies. Policies on the development of social media are limited but should not go beyond IT in terms of development of the use or reproduction of content, and have to observe the boundaries imposed by religious and cultural resistance. So before the development of the Internet in the area, both production procedures and information in all sectors must be organised to meet the requirements of exchangeable standards in a network, and very considerable funds allocated to this. It is essential to upgrade legislative requirements in the field of network communications.

These laws, in particular those regarding reproduction rights and the ownership of cultural artefacts, software and electronic data, have the overwhelming effect of encouraging cultural production on the network. Cultural policy should encourage the use of technology by cultural institutions and seek to optimise their impact on the target audience, though it is not clear whether any use of the new technology will necessarily lead to an increase in influence on audiences. Cultural monitoring systems based on the exchange of data content and national registers of data and databases have an essential role in preventing the spread of corruption, security threats, electronic breaches and psychological operations. The next challenge Middle Eastern countries face in the era of information technology is the use of Persian and Arabic on the net. From a sociologist's point of view, language is the most important and most basic cultural icon in a community. In terms of orientation towards the international community, all countries are trying to share their cultural products through the network, and language plays a key role in paving the way. That is why it is essential that the Persian and Arabic languages and cultures have a strong presence on the net, in order to increase the numbers having access to social media. The next strategy is to move towards the privatisation of IT and to set up policies on communication and surveillance in these areas rather than leaving the whole process of the production and dissemination of information in the hands of the government (Tabatabaeian, 2009). Common indicators of information technology in Middle Eastern states suggest that, despite the fact that in many of these countries economic development programmes emphasise the downsizing of the public sector, research results show that the size of government may not decrease, but may actually increase instead. This may be due to the limited transfer of state enterprises to the private sector or the establishment of new companies in the public sector. Government must make sensible decisions so that at least one of the two scenarios cannot transpire, extending the transfer or establishing smaller companies in the public sector. The next factor may be the creation of a database of full citizens. It is true that there are many democracies in developing countries, as well as closer monitoring of citizens, because there is a strong database of all the income indicators, such as living standards for the people, etc. but the lack of adequate infrastructure in the Middle East was not monitored every time. The next solution would be to create a comprehensive national system of innovation in the field of social media and to make better use of social media as a tool set to improve the system described. Social media can be used to install and maintain democracy and social justice at the heart of society and can support people in functioning in all areas, especially economics.

In the national innovation system, in order to raise people's awareness of information technology, entrepreneurship education based on social media, the creation of knowledge sharing between supply chains and the creation of a system of ideas can help the social media. In fact, in terms of a resource-based theory, knowledge could take the place of other resources. The traditional tools developed in the Middle East have survived but are old and unsatisfying. All the parts of the system are separated and social media may be the easiest way to connect them. The next step is to reconcile family culture with the essential concepts of social media. It is essential, of course, to create an environment in which all religious groups and all Western-oriented groups can take advantage of the media. The use of social media is so widespread that, instead of trying to avoid media penetration, religious groups in Islamic countries and elsewhere should be more active in the media, to balance the formation of this competitive system. Here again the role of training becomes more important.

If people know that building a broad-based system for monitoring the government through social media can reduce or increase the legitimacy of the government, the potential of the media obviously becomes more and more evident to the people. The government will be more responsible to the people and the people will have confidence in the safety of cyberspace and know their virtual rights. Thus, when one uses information technology to tackle the field of corruption, the first big steps toward establishing democracy and social justice will have been taken. Finally, the experts emphasise the creation of a development field for venture capital, to improve the quality and quantity of social media investment. Even if the government fails to execute their private duties well, they can encourage the presence of VCs, thus solving an important proportion of the economic and social problems in developing countries, because in addition to providing finance, such companies can play an important role in developing a culture of entrepreneurship and transferring management experience to start-up companies.

Samad Aghaei, in his paper of 2004, considered the following problems in the development of the VC industry:

1. Lack of security and economic stability.
2. Lack of a national system of innovation.
3. Change of government, state monopolies and lack of sufficient attention to small-scale industry.
4. Lack of adequate knowledge of the planners, policy-makers and government officials to the industry.
5. Lack of laws and regulations to protect the VC industry and the official custodian of the industry.
6. Lack of association among universities, industry, research and development centres, incubators, science parks, technology companies, and venture capitalists and business angels.
7. Lack of transparent, accurate and up-to-date financial information.
8. Inability to attract foreign venture capital investment companies in Iran.
9. Negative thinking towards bankruptcy with bankrupts regarded as vulgar and doomed people.
10. Lack of familiarity with the industry's entrepreneurs.

Young companies have difficulty attracting elite and professional staff, but VCs can use their fame and their various relationships to help them. VCs can provide value added with high quality, and indeed will enjoy a sustainable competitive advantage against other investors. The VCs and financial intermediaries, shareholders and investors need mechanisms that enable them to get a return on their investment. Therefore, it is reasonable that VCs invest only when they can predict the direction of the return on their investment (Metrick and Yasuda, 2010). So the lack of an exit route for companies that invest in information technology and social media in the Middle East is an important factor that should be considered by policy-makers in creating a safe environment for such companies, the state guaranteeing their long-term profit.

Overall conclusion

This book has been written over a period of over two and a half years, and during the writing a lot of changes have taken place in the countries studied, the speed of which was much greater than can be dealt with in this book. However, in the author's opinion, the social media were not able to play a beneficial role because the media cover so broad a field that virtually any group of actors can achieve all their goals in the social media and change government policy in their favour. We can say that this outcome is virtually inevitable because no part of it is uncontrollable policy, and even with appropriate policy and conditions favouring slight adjustments there is still no guarantee of success. We will update the book and include the new experiences gained from the Arab Spring. The author, like any other Muslim, hopes this Arab Spring will eventually establish peace, security and solidarity in the countries surveyed and that the headless revolutions in the social media do not simply become a bad memory.

In any case, it is too early now to judge the success of social media in promoting democracy and social justice. We have seen so far at least that the social media in countries that already enjoy peace and prosperity neither increase nor decrease welfare but have roughly the same advantages and disadvantages as were already present. However, countries suffering under poverty and tyranny are still not getting a satisfactory result. Perhaps we need to go back to the point where social media may well be located in countries in which, owing to the lack of a culture of technology and other issues discussed in this chapter, corruption and tyranny are the perfect tools for the state, so that other methods must be sought. However, we should not ignore the fact that in the medium term the media have been partially effective in offsetting policy in Iran and Saudi Arabia; those governments will create changes in their policies to increase citizen satisfaction with the physical environment before it can be controlled in the virtual environment.

References

Bayo-Moriones, A., & Lera-Lopez, F. (2007). A firm-level analysis of determinants of ICT adoption in Spain. *Technovation, 27*(6−7), 352−366.

Ghazinouri Naeini, R., & Tavakol, M. (2011). Diffusion and obstacles to ICT adoption in Iranian industries: Case study of selected sectors. *Journal of Science and Technology Policy, 3*(2), 31−45.

Metrick, A., & Yasuda, A. (2010). *Venture capital and finance of innovation* (2nd ed.). John Wiley & Sons.

Rashidirad, M., Elahi, S., & Hasanzadeh, A. (2009). Key issues in IS management in Iran and variables that affect them. *Journal of Science and Technology Policy, 1*(4), 21−37.

Potnis, D. (2010). Measuring e-governance as an innovation in the public sector. *Government Information Quarterly, 27*(1).

Samad Aghaei, J. (2004). *Venture capital industry as infrastructure of national innovation system*, First National Conference on Venture Capital Industry, Tehran, Iran (In Persian).

Tabatabaeian, S. H. (2009). *Study, identification and analysis of current situation and designing desirable situation of Iran technology and comparative analysis with selected countries: Analytical report of information and communication technology* (1st ed.). Tehran: Allameh Tabatabaei University.

Index

Printed in the United States
By Bookmasters